Dear Andrew

I hope

read!

MAKE MINE A MEDIUM

Prophecy & Spiritual Insights of a Clairvoyant Psychic Medium

Jeff Hewitt

Jeff Hewitt

First Edition: 2024

www.JeffHewittMedium.com

ISBN: 978-1-0686481-0-6

DISCLAIMER

This book is intended for informational and entertainment purposes only. The views and opinions expressed herein are solely those of the author and do not necessarily reflect those of the publisher or any affiliated parties.

While real experiences inspire many of the stories and anecdotes within this book, certain names, characters, places, and incidents have been modified or used fictitiously for privacy and narrative purposes. Any resemblance to actual persons, living or dead, businesses, companies, events, or locales is purely coincidental.

The content of this book does not constitute professional advice. The psychic readings, experiences, and adventures described are based on the author's personal interpretations and experiences and should not be taken as factual or scientific. Readers are advised to use their discretion and judgment while interpreting the contents of this book.

ACKNOWLEDGMENTS

This book contains many threads of insight and inspiration and without the help of others' valuable and rich contributions, it would not have made it into print.

Thank you to Julie Soskin and Sharry Clarke as my main evening class tutors without which my unfoldment would not have been possible.

Thank you to Judith Seelig for the spiritual holidays, and Ian Galloway for giving me the encouragement to carry the book forward.

Thanks also to the late Mary Armour and to Derek Robinson for believing in me and for giving me great encouragement and support along the way.

Huge thanks to Grace Fleming who painstakingly typed up all of my notes, some written years ago to form the book. Thanks a million, you are a brick.

Special thanks to the editor Jo Ward whose critical eye and constructive feedback helped tremendously to hone and polish the book to what it is now; also for your technical advice.

I would also like to thank spiritual readers, Dawn, Shirley, Paula, and Susan.

Each and every one of you, has left an indelible mark on this book and I am very grateful to you.

Thank you very much!

CONTENTS

PROLOGUE

The metallic clank of the letterbox flap awoke me in my small, sparsely furnished, first-floor bedroom. Apart from a few well-thumbed, jet-lagged letters from Australia, and the far too regular bills, my correspondence rarely troubled the London postman, so I descended the stairs fully expecting to find yet another letter addressed to my flatmate in Battersea.

The handwritten name staring up from the padded envelope was mine. I lifted the package from the mat and explored the parcel with my fingers. The only thing that I could deduce was that it had been sent from here in the UK, so it wasn't a late Christmas present. Not being blessed with my eldest sister's uncanny knack for guessing the contents of gifts, I gave up and resorted to route one, and ripped the package open!

Inside was a cassette. There was nothing else, no note or explanation either. Then I remembered exactly what it was. Months earlier, I met a spiritual medium at a workshop I attended. We had got talking, and she seemed to take a shine to me, saying that before the start of each year, she always did a practice reading in order to reconnect with the spirit people.

Her new term must have been about to start, as she asked if I would like a free reading. I had jumped at the offer, and now here I was, months later, turning the tape that contained it over in my hands.

I was amazed! How could this lady read me when I had met her so briefly, so long ago, and most remarkable of all, when I had not even been with her when she did it! As I went upstairs, the extraordinary incidents that had led me to that workshop, led me to where I was today, even who I was today, came flooding back to me. I went over to the cassette player, inserted the tape, and settled myself down to listen to the reading. I had no idea what was in store for me. I put the kettle on.

PART ONE

To my Maternal Grandmother, Thelma Elizabeth Sanders nee Daddow.

Chapter One

SPIRITUAL AWAKENINGS

New Year's Day, 2024

"I work with the dead!" he announced, unprompted by me. I raised my eyebrows, "What in a mortuary? I asked, "Well, I hope you washed your hands!" I quipped as he handed me the pint over the bar. Well, I guess you've seen the odd limb move and heard some strange sounds, I said, half inviting him to tell me a funny and grotesque story! "I've seen it all ", he said brashly. I wondered to myself if he told everyone who came into the pub what his other job was?

I thought I would give as good as I got, "I work with the dead too! I announced. I work with the spirits of dead people." He gave me a look.

Really? He said and then went on to say, "I went to a theatre to see one, she was useless! My friend had committed suicide and she couldn't even bring him through". "It doesn't work like that," I said honestly.

"Now show me what you've got!" He had thrown down the gauntlet! "Well, I'm not switched on," I said defensively, feeling put on the spot, "I have to be in the zone ". I sipped my drink.

I didn't want to shirk the request, so I linked in. "Well, you have a Collie dog around you." I said, "I'm not sure who it belonged to, you or someone around you, but its spirit is here!" He gave me a look. Tell me more, he said!

"I see a lady who likes flowers, she is showing me a carnation. There is a wedding coming up!" You're good he announced!

"Now, do you want some feedback?"

He pulled his T-shirt sleeve up to reveal a tattoo of a dog on his shoulder. This was my dog, he said. My cousin is getting married next month.

"Now I want more!" He demanded! "Oh, I have to sing for my supper," I bantered back.

I linked back in. "Ashes" I said, someone has someone's ashes. That certain someone can't make up their mind where to spread them. He filled me in. "My sister has Dad's ashes, and she doesn't know." I carried on, "Well she has decided somewhere recently, and the man in spirit approves!" I gave him quite a reading. He kept saying, I want more! It wasn't what I had expected to do on New Year's Day!

A Different College, 1995

There is an institution in London called The College of Psychic Studies, which, among other things, holds weekend workshops. They like somebody to do door duty, a role which involves ticking off workshop attendees as they arrive and stopping any strangers from entering the college building. So, on some of my weekends, I played the role of an unofficial security guard. The pay-off was one free workshop in exchange for four-door duties. For someone with no spare money and a thirst for spiritual knowledge, this was a great trade-off. I would carefully study the college's catalogue in order to choose which workshop to enrol in after my four-door duties had been banked.

The workshop I had chosen on this particular occasion was titled "Being Open to a Spiritual Life." On the second day, a lovely lady I had met there, called Anne, passed to me a few hand-written pages.

"Here you are," she said, as though this was the most natural thing in the world! "Here are some channelled notes I wrote on the train on the way here for you!" I was so chuffed. Don't get the wrong idea, they weren't love notes, but I felt so special, having seemingly been chosen from any number of people who were attending the two-day event. Here were three pages of channelled writings.

My life had switched from the usual to the unusual. Previously, I would spend my time working, seeing friends, going to the cinema, attending the occasional birthday party, meeting colleagues for a drink after work, lying in the park, or going for a swim. The exact same thing that almost every other 28-year-old would fill their days, weeks and months up with.

It all happened within the space of a day, a twenty-four-hour period that would completely change the direction my life was travelling in and, in so doing, change my life forever. I had a series of spontaneous paranormal experiences. Incidents that stopped as suddenly as they had started, but ones that set me on a path of questions and led me to look at life in a completely different light, examining it using a whole new language: a spiritual one. This is from someone who was simply unaware of spiritual oneness within life and the energy behind all life.

Happenings

The orange river of lava snaked its way down the slope, following the contours of the earth in what usually held a small stream, causing a hissing sound as the two elements met.

In the distance, the moonlight showed up a wooden hut downstream. Smoke coming from the chimney meant that the hut was occupied! At its current rate, it would be 15 minutes before the lava reached the cabin.

It was a hut for trackers, and I had made the long haul up the mountainside that day, having chosen a solitary walking holiday for that Easter break. With a long day ahead of me for the next day I had gone to bed early. I was tucked up in the wooden bunk bed of roughly hewn timber planks, in my sleeping bag, with a yoga mat as my soft mattress! It didn't take me long to drift off to sleep. Ironically, I found gazing at the orange embers in the fireplace a cosy comfort as I drifted off to sleep. I remember dreaming, of all things, of cows on a grassy mountainside in Switzerland!

The dream changed, and a grass fire spread up the slope, causing them to stampede. One cow came straight at me, and I woke up with a start. I noticed immediately that something was wrong; the hut had become stiflingly hot. I sat up and looked around the simply furnished hut. There was an orange glow mirrored upon the widow pane! I quickly unzipped my sleeping bag and jumped to the floor. I couldn't believe how warm it had become. I took a few steps to the door, glancing quickly at my watch. It was 3 in the morning, and I grabbed the door handle, only to let it go as it was hot!

I leant back, grabbed my sleeping bag, and used it as an oven glove on the door. A wave of intense heat blasted towards me as I flung the door open and saw the orange river of lava in front of me; I'm going to burn alive!

I sat bolt upright in bed, sweat pouring from my brow! I looked at my watch, 03:01! I looked around my dark London room, realising it was a dream, a dream within a dream!

Wow, that was vivid, I thought; what had triggered that nightmare? I wondered.

I could hear a police siren in the distance, a familiar London sound; it was unusually reassuring. I checked that my alarm was set for 6.30 and settled back down to sleep, wondering how my mind could be so lucid!

At 6.30, I went straight into my morning rhythm of showering, dressing, breakfast, making a packed lunch, feeding the cat, and cleaning my teeth on autopilot to leave for work. As I was leaving, my phone beeped; damn, I thought as I read the text message, the driver of a team wasn't going to make it in; he was sick that day, the text said. I texted his teammate to go directly to the site, and I soon had a text back asking me if I could collect his work boots from the van. After a couple of other text messages, I jumped in my van and drove off to collect his boots.

I turned on the radio; it was the morning news. "At 3 in the morning, Mount Etna, in Sicily, had erupted," that's odd, I thought, immediately remembering my lava dream from exactly the same time in the morning. "Gosh", I thought, "Was that just a coincidence, or was my dream predictive?" The hairs stood up on the back of my neck! I changed channels for some cheery morning pop!

The sick driver lived at the same end of London, so it didn't take too long before I pulled up outside his house.

I rang the doorbell, and the door opened a crack with the keys being passed through. We exchanged some brief pleasantries, with his front door being a go-between, and I strode off to the Sherpa van. I unlocked the driver's side door and jumped in, sitting in his seat. I immediately saw the boots on the passenger's side floor. I reached over to collect them.

As I took hold of them, I suddenly felt a wave of energy, like a force field encompass me. It felt slow but couldn't have lasted more than a second or two. This cocoon of energy completely enveloped me! Suddenly, I "BECAME" the driver, the sick chap! My personality changed. I was a little jealous. I experienced a whole new set of emotions. What was happening to me? How could I become someone else? I seemed to have picked his energy off the van seat! How could that be possible?

This chap had always been "Boss resistant"; I suspected him to be a little envious, as I was his boss and a lot younger than him. This was not a harmony of emotion! I quickly exited the van; I felt odd. Slowly, the sensations faded away as I came back to myself.

When I felt confident everything was ok, I walked back to his front door, pushed the keys through the letterbox, and returned to the van. I scratched my head.

I remembered the volcanos, and now this! What was going on? Am I going crazy today? I hadn't had a boozy weekend. I never took drugs. What was going on?

I drove on to the first job and gave the other chap his boots. "Are you ok?" he said. You are as white as a sheet! I'm fine I said, glossing it over. There was a normal working day ahead of me, so I carried on as usual on the outside, determined to plough my physical self into my usual work, but despite that, my mind raced!

The gardening day went on without event, and I heaved a sigh of relief as the time came to go home. I packed up my gardening tools and bags of green waste and stacked them into the van. I headed back home. The job was physically taxing, and it was a strenuous day.

I pulled into the "residents only" parking bay space and settled back into my garden flat in Tufnell Park, feeling a sense of normality return. I had already sent the others their week's rota and provided that the sick chap was better, the week should go without a hitch. I put my dinner in the oven, showered and turned the TV on, all set for a night to recharge my batteries. I fed my cat and saw that I was out of milk. I needed my breakfast cereal at the start of the day too, and so did my cat need its milk!

So I set off to the end of the street to fetch a pint of milk. Tufnell Park was a quiet part of London, very middle class and apparently "up and coming", the estate agent had told me when I had bought it. Off I went to get the milk, walking to the end of the road and then taking a left to get to the corner store near to the tube station.

As I rounded the corner onto the much busier main road, a young chap was walking my way. With both of us minding our own business, we passed each other on the pavement. Wallop! Suddenly, I was cocooned with his energy! The same thing was happening to me as in the morning! In an instant, I became this chap! I was a very different person. I was aggressive and itching for a fight! If I had a baseball bat, goodness only knows what I would have wanted to do with it! I wanted to hit someone!

It was so much the opposite of my personality that I knew this chap was sparring for a fight. His energy hung around me like treacle!

I sent up a prayer: Dear Lord, what is happening to me? Help me, Lord! Am I going crazy?

At the time, reflecting on these three incidents, my overriding thought was, "I'm going mad. Why am I having these experiences?" I started to read spiritual books, searching for an answer. I read books such as Paramhansa Yogananda's "Autobiography of a Yogi" and various self-improvement books. These experiences were not merely a case of daydreaming; they were so much more than that. I had not been under the influence of any drugs or alcohol. I was in my late twenties; what was happening to me?

While in the middle of "Autobiography of a Yogi", my thoughts were centred around what I was reading, what had happened to me recently and how they related to each other. I was taking one day at that time, and as I was driving through the ring road at Regents Park, pondering a question that was related to all of those three, when all of a sudden, a strange feeling came over me, and I received an answer to the question. It dropped into my mind. Then I received another answer, a higher answer, which, without the first one, the second would have made no sense. Then I received a third answer, and again, without the first two answers, this would have made no sense. More answers came, one after another. It was like climbing a ladder, each rung another answer, a higher and higher truth. Up the ladder I climbed until I received the ultimate answer to the question, the highest truth. I could only hold each answer in my mind for an instant as it was above and beyond my normal comprehension. As each answer passed through my mind, I would have a moment of understanding, and then it would be gone, to be replaced by the next one.

When the final answer came, and I received what I knew was the ultimate truth to my initial question, it was accompanied by another feeling, one of bliss. My dazzled brain searched around for something to cling to. Was this God? This feeling of bliss stayed with me for days. I was certain that I had been touched by something divine and holy, something way beyond my norm. The feeling of euphoria may have persisted, but the answers and, indeed, the question had disappeared from my grasp almost as soon as I had received them. I felt that I was not ready; I just wasn't prepared or capable of taking on all this information. It was like putting 150 watts into a 20-watt bulb. I wasn't that evolved!

A few days later, I was working again near Regent's Park, this time in Park Village West. Often, for lunch, I would go to an Italian delicatessen in Parkway. On this particular day, I ordered spaghetti Bolognese. I patiently waited for my order, gazing out the window as the black cabs trundled past. My eyes focused on one particular taxi. Suddenly, I started to feel weird. I was overcome by an energy that blanketed and engulfed me.

I found myself going back in time, the pace of my journey becoming faster and faster as I went past all the wars, all the good and all the bad, back and back in time to its dawn, to the emergence of life on earth, where the world was dark and covered with oceans, the only living thing was algae in the water. Then I was thrust back to the present to the exact moment the taxi I had been focussing on passed by the café's window. Like before, I felt blissed out. Everything was sacred; everything was perfect, both the bad and the good. All was an experience and part of God, ultimately. The cab driving down the street was a divine event. Every single thing and every single moment is completely divine and sacred, all a part of a divine universe.

My spaghetti arrived. Had I just slipped into a trance? What was happening to me? I was being bombarded with esoteric experiences. I ate the spaghetti and returned to work, still in a state of euphoria. It was like before; the by-product of truth was bliss.

I went to an alternative healer, told him what had happened to me, and asked why these things were occurring. At this point, I still wasn't sure whether I was becoming enlightened or simply going mad! The healer confessed that he did not know what these were or what they meant, but he did know that people in the spirit movement would give their eye teeth for just one of these experiences!

Frustrated at this lack of help, I kept looking for answers in the books I was reading. I read many books. There came a point when I realised they were ultimately all saying the same thing, 'LOVE YOURSELF'. The problem was, though, that they didn't tell you how to go about achieving it, I had thought. One of the books I had read was from an alternative doctor who worked at a well-known London alternative healing centre, The Hale Clinic, just by Regents Park. Her book had only just been published, so I was hopeful that she should very much have her "finger on the spiritual pulse", as it were; I wondered if she was the person who could help me and give me the answers I was so desperate to learn.

I took myself to the Hale Clinic, which is not far from Harley Street. It seemed to be the alternatives equivalent and a place where many alternative health practitioners at the top of their field hold weekly clinics. I made an appointment to see the doctor. It turned out she was also an iridologist, and I found myself having my eyeballs scanned!

"Well, you are always going for gold," she said, "so I'll give you some", she explained, administering the homoeopathic remedy for such a thing before sending me on my way.

"Now, hang on a minute!" I exclaimed as it seemed my appointment was over all too quickly! I explained to her that I had been having spiritual experiences and visions and asked her what I should do about them. Without any hesitation and with a straightforward certainty, she gave me my answer.

"Go to the College of Psychic Studies and see Julie Soskin." She didn't want to hear any more about me or my experiences and sent me on my way once again. At that time, I needed to believe in someone. I needed something to hang onto, a handrail to lead me onwards, and I had the first step at last! The doctor had said it with such certainty that I was sure I finally had my lead to explain what on earth was going on.

At last, I was on my way, and I felt a sense of relief. I had the name of someone who could help me. I immediately called the College of Psychic Studies in Queensbury Place for an appointment with Julie Soskin. Luck was on my side; the new term was due to start shortly, and they were finalising numbers for each class, so I didn't have to wait long for an appointment.

As the day of the interview approached, I found myself becoming more and more nervous. I had never met a medium before and I had no idea what to expect or what I was letting myself in for. Was this another step on an extraordinary journey that I had neither planned nor felt prepared for? A journey to... I had absolutely no idea to where!

I remember thinking that with just one glance, she would be able to see right through me, right inside me, and hence know all about me, things I didn't even know myself. Little did I know then that it doesn't work like that.

The day came, and I took myself off to South Kensington station and then walked for five minutes to Queensbury Place. Arriving early for my 'interview', which I had been informed was given on an 'invitation only' basis, I walked up the steps of the period property into what once must have been a private house. In the corridor was a leaflet rack stacked with pamphlets of upcoming events. On the other side of the corridor, it must have been knocked out sometime before to make way for a set of double doors that led into a large reception area boasting a long wooden desk, behind which no less than three receptionists sat.

"I'm here to meet Julie," I told all three of them nervously.

I was asked to wait in the library, which was in the remainder of the ground floor. I wandered around the bookshelves, looking at the titles, before pulling something off the shelf and taking a seat. My mind was too preoccupied with what was to come to do anything more than absently thumb through the book and pretend to read the sepia-coloured pages. A little while later, I was asked to go upstairs to the third floor, where I was to wait in a wooden chair in the hall until Julie was ready for me. When a short blonde lady in her late thirties came out to usher me into her office, the first thing I thought was, "She looks very normal!" The next thing I thought was that "she was looking directly into my soul!" It was unnerving.

Julie was very relaxed. Again, the meeting took only a few minutes. I explained that I had been having spiritual experiences and that the doctor had said I should see her. This seemed to clinch it. Like with the doctor, Julie didn't ask me about my experiences; it didn't matter. She remarked that I was very intuitive and told me I was accepted into the psychic development class at the College of Psychic Studies. Wow! I couldn't believe that 'Gardening Jeff' from Tasmania was about to embark on such an extraordinary endeavour. It also meant that, finally, I would get my answers and have everything I had been going through explained to me. I could not wait.

Early Life

Perhaps I was always a spiritual person, underneath my normal existence as a regular guy. I had left Tasmania when I was nearly 19 to take up a new life in the UK, following my instincts after feeling a pull from this island on the other side of the globe, even though it was a wrench for me to leave my family and, no doubt, a wrench for them too.

Despite all that I had ever known was Australia, the country had always felt somehow foreign to me. Then, when my plane flew over the London cityscape and landed at Heathrow, my overriding sense was that I had come home. It was deeper than merely feeling that this was the land of my ancestors. The only other person who I knew felt the same as I did was my best friend from school. Every other white Australian were very much in the patriotic Aussie camp, with most making sure everyone else was fully aware of the fact. Knowing what I know now, I would say that I have had past lives in Britain, and for that reason, it was easier for me to uproot from my life in Tasmania and to follow my destiny. England was the place where I was to fulfil that destiny.

I started my earliest days on Flinders Island, which is a small island between Tasmania and the Australian mainland. Its population was primarily made up of descendants from the colonial sealing days and their Aboriginal partners, land grant war veterans who went on to become farmers and a smattering of other farmers who had bought in. My father went there to advise on better farming methods through a government posting. Prior to white-man settlement, Flinders Island was uninhabited. In the 1830s, the last of the Tasmanian Aborigines were rounded up and re-homed on the island with the promise that they would return one day to their homeland. Their numbers dwindled as they succumbed to white man's diseases, which they had little or no immunity to. Eventually, the last handful were resettled near to the Tasmanian capital, Hobart.

Tasmania was a wonderful place to grow up in. My mother would take us out every weekend to experience the incredible nature that was all around us. Whether that be on a walk through a tree fern forest with myrtle trees to a stunning waterfall with yellow-tailed cockatoos keeping us company along the way, into the bush for a BBQ with a circle of gathered stones for the frying pan and "Billy", a tin saucepan for boiling water, or climbing a mountain, walking for miles along one of the numerous pristine and empty beaches. They were happy-go-lucky days for me as a child, even though these trips would only be allowed after the Sunday morning church service, choir practice and hours and hours of school homework! I didn't enjoy school, especially as I got older and it became more and more cliquey. Despite that, I got good grades, and it was expected that I would go on to further education. I started my A levels, but after a term, I decided to leave, something my mother wasn't too happy about. Like so many people at that age, I didn't know what I wanted to do when I "grew up".

My parents split up when I was seven, and my mother had her hands full raising us children as a lone parent with little to no money. It must have been incredibly tough for her, but she did a wonderful job. With things as they are now, I think she was a woman well before her time.

My mother's people were from farming stock on the Victorian wheat belt, just outside a town called Horsham. When she first split from my father we went and lived with her parents for a year. As there were 5 of us, we took it in turns to be billeted out to nearby Aunts and Uncles until a house was found. Perhaps everybody in her hometown were judging her for being a divorced mother, or simply for the fact that her marriage had not worked out. I don't know. But I remember as a child thinking it was a very good thing when they divorced as they were so unsuited to each other!

My mother chose to move to the Tasmanian town of Devonport when she returned from Victoria. I recall a promontory there simply called "The Bluff". This was one place where we played as children. There were large stones with Aboriginal rock carvings, usually taking the form of large circles carved into the rock.

During my childhood, all my brothers and sisters would give each other nicknames. Mine was Sook Magrook, while my siblings went under the aliases of Marie the Wee, Poker McGroker, Michelle the Smell and Liar Magriar. I still can't decide if I came out better off or worse than the rest!

When I was around nine, I made a best friend at school. He had just arrived from the Gold Coast. His parents had been "Ten Pound Poms", a term given to British immigrants to Australia after the Second World War due to the £10 processing fee they were charged. He was very proud of his English ancestry. We had many boyhood adventures together and were very much the "Terrible Two". Though we were generally considered very good, and essentially we were, we were still young boys and got up to plenty of harmless mischief! Indeed, we had a great laugh, and my memories of that time are full of fun and happiness, our stomachs aching from laughing so much because of our silly jokes.

I must have been about 12 years old when my father and his new wife bought a farm, where they set about growing flowers on a commercial level for florists. Along with one of my brothers, I would go there in the school holidays. My other three siblings were older and somehow missed the school holiday visits. I remember returning from one of these visits with 12 chrysanthemum cuttings. My mother's house had a large backyard with just a patch of grass. I dug out a square beside the side fence and planted the "chrysies", as we called them. I lovingly nurtured them, and when Mother's Day came, I put an advert in the local paper and sold 20 bunches. My father and his new wife couldn't work out how I managed to get 20 bunches from 12 plants!

I had an interest in plants from that point on, and I tended a few bonsai trees, carefully trimming their leaves with a pair of nail scissors. I entered a native bonsai I had rescued from a rock, and before long got first prize. My success with the chrysies inspired me, though, and before long, I had dug up a swathe of my mother's backyard and set about making a garden. The house was on a large plot, and apart from a small shed in one corner and an aviary that my grandfather had built for my mother on one of his trips from the mainland, there was nothing else.

My next project was to dig out and concrete a pond. I kept having an idea to lower an area of the garden and build a path that would go through this lower section. Still, I questioned myself as to why I had come up with such an idea, as surely it would simply fill with water in the winter. Now, all these years later, I understand that Gertrude Jekyll, a renowned British garden designer from the 1900s, had a penchant for a sunken garden! I had just read the book, "An English Ladies Garden" and one of her gardens was in the book.

The new garden was complete with raised beds and a pond. It would be illegal now, but we went down to the beach and carted back stones for the raised beds in mum's car boot. I filled the garden with flowers. I'd come home from school and tend to the garden when perhaps I should have been concentrating on my homework. I did manage to find time for my schoolwork, but my heart was never in it, and when I left college, I went to work on my father's flower farm, much to my mother's disappointment that I didn't further my education.

Chapter Two

UNFOLDMENT

I left work early and took the London underground to the Psychic College in Kensington. It is in a very smart part of town. Actually, I don't think anywhere in Kensington isn't smart! I had no idea what to expect from the class, but after my experiences, I thought I was in the right place and was now heading in the right direction to where I would find some answers and, hopefully, all would be explained.

I had been counting down the days for the class to start, and now, finally, here I was, sitting in a circle of about eight people. I felt like a complete beginner and an outsider! It was as though I had never experienced any of those strange happenings. I was starting from scratch.

I attended once a week, and it was such a strange experience. It was like everyone was using a whole different language from one that I knew, but they were using it as if it were the most normal and natural thing in the world.

"I see a green light around you," one would say. I would open an eye and take a peek, but no matter how much I squinted or stared, I couldn't see the green light!

"You have Archangel Michael with you." Was another one. Me? Really? Where? Others were even more leftfield. An animal totem, auras, different planes of existence... even different times! This was seriously wacky. One woman even told me that when I entered a garden, the plants were filled with joy! After my strange experiences, I thought I would feel at home and all would become clear, but this was something else entirely.

Typically, the classes would start with a guided meditation to open ourselves and our energies up to the spiritual dimension. This was all done with our imaginations. We would do different exercises each week, all with our eyes shut. It was very interactive, with each of us having to relate to whom we were paired up with or to the whole class what we had received from the exercise through our minds.

The first exercise in the class was always to 'open up'; as the evening class finished, we did one to 'close down'. I seemed to get one thing correct every week that could be validated by another member of the group. This kept me going and kept me excited, too. Gone were all of my Jesus-like experiences! Now, I was a beginner, learning a new language from scratch, a language of spirit.

Working with the Land

Running a small garden maintenance business and having to pay the bills certainly kept me grounded, if you pardon the pun. Excited as I was, there was no chance to be 'away with the fairies.'

In London, I had become self-employed, maintaining gardens, after working for Clifton Nurseries, a well-known London garden centre considered to be the 'Harrods' of garden centres. It was an invaluable experience and it was there that I learnt much of my UK plant knowledge.

After that, I worked for two garden maintenance companies for six months each before I realised I could and should do it myself. I had one job to start with that I had initially been doing on weekends, where I would get the train from Homerton to Camden Road and then walk to the garden on the edge of Regent's Park. Luckily, I wasn't paying too much rent and just managed to scrape by on that income.

Soon after starting, the neighbour's gardener quit, so I got to work on that garden as well, which made the commute much nicer!

The Regents Park garden was in an impressive enclave of about 12 detached villas designed by Robert Nash. In times gone by there had been a canal at the bottom of the garden, an extension of the Regents Canal, but with that waterway no longer there, it meant these addresses enjoyed very large gardens.

Another job I got was a one-off clearance for a lady in West Hampstead. It turned out that she held yoga classes for the St. John's Wood ladies 'set' and she was very happy for me to put my business card on her notice board. That provided a huge boost and in no time at all. I received several more gardens to work on. Word started to spread, and before too long, I had to buy a vehicle. I saw a covered ute (sorry, some of my Australian heritage has stayed with me!) advertised for £300 in High Wycombe, got the train there and bought it. I was then up and running as a gardening business.

It wasn't too long before clients were asking for me to re-design parts of their garden. I had not studied any design, and at Clifton, I was the shop manager's assistant. A client in Hamilton Terrace, one of North London's premier roads had a path to her front door and just an awkward bank of earth leading to her front basement window. She asked me to come up with a design. I stood there with pad and pen in hand, gazing at the pile of earth. In a flash, I saw the whole thing completed in my mind's eye! Relying on my technical drawing lessons from high school, I drew what I had envisioned: complicated terracing with curved brick levels that divided the space into three levels.

That little garden is still there today, some 30 years on! Where did my instant flash of the whole garden come from? I scratched my head again in disbelief but went with it.

Insight

I would count the days down to the class. It was the highlight of my week.

After several months, Julie announced that we would link to the spirit world and bring somebody through who had passed away! I had no idea what to expect and was still very 'green' but as one thing could be validated each week, I was certainly willing to give everything a try.

I followed the 'opening up' visualisation to allow my energies in to the spiritual dimension. I took my energy above my head with the faculty of my imagination and saw a blank screen in front of me, like a TV screen with the volume turned down. We had been paired off for this, and it was my turn to 'read' for my partner.

"What do you see?" came their question.

I focussed my thoughts on the blank screen. It remained blank for a second or two, and then suddenly, I saw a yacht sailing in the ocean. The sea was rough, and the yacht quickly sank. That was all that I saw before the screen in my mind went completely blank again. I opened my eyes and told my partner, who was from New Zealand, what I had seen.

"I knew somebody who drowned at sea in a yacht," was all she said.

I nearly skipped all the way home, amazed that I had mentioned someone from the spirit side of life, excited even though the circumstances had been far from nice. Fortunately, I saw it detached from all emotion, or I imagine it would have been a far less pleasing experience. This experience was a form of clairvoyance I was told.

I found the classes so exciting. I was fascinated by what people told me or what I could get myself or relay to somebody else. My confidence grew, and very slowly, I began to receive more and more information. I was very committed and soaked it all up like a sponge. I learnt that there were other ways of picking up the information. I could feel something as though it were real, like a mini version of my first experiences. I learnt from the others that one could hear things also, while one lady used to smell things. With some, the intuition, simply a knowing, was how they received information.

After a while, Julie moved away from the college and set up her own psychic school. All my classmates followed her, as did I. My new journey to class meant getting the train to Richmond and walking up Church Hill to St. Matthias church at the top of the hill. This impressive building, whose spire could be seen for miles around, had rooms that were rented out. Another class was held on the other side of the church and led by another medium, Penny Brown John. Also, her Husband, Rupert, would teach spiritual healing. They called their new school "Insight & Intuition."

As before, Julie did something different in every class. In one particular week, we were to do channelling. Julie always led the opening up and meditations and monitored the proceedings. She then explained what we would do. On this occasion, we were to hold the energy above our heads and, at the given moment, just let the words tumble out without thinking about it, not letting our minds come onto it. We were to link to the highest possible light force. This was another new experience for me, and I did my best to still my mind and take the energy above my head. Julie went around the group one by one. From memory a variety of information came through from the people in the class, about angels to starlight and universal energy. It was difficult to leave one's mind open without the conscious thought about what one would say to jump in.

At last, it came round to me, and a few words tumbled out.

"Align yourself to the light, or you will burn." That was it, nothing more. I was mortified. Everybody else seemed to channel positive and uplifting information. Mine was anything but that and seemed to be a stark warning. Looking back now, I believe it was channelled from a higher power, as mankind has largely not aligned itself, and society as a whole often focuses on the wrong priorities. I didn't like the words I channelled, so I put them to the back of my mind and carried on with the other exercises. Julie didn't comment. The other participants channelled golden light and an angel, joyful in contrast to the stark words.

I went through a period of questioning the exercises we did in class, or the circle as it was known, questioning what good it was doing and wondering how it could help in 'real life'. It was all a bit wacky and not something that would be considered cool by any stretch of the imagination. I hadn't mentioned it to any of my friends as I knew they would think it was all too weird. As there had been mental health problems within my family, I also decided not to didn't mention it to my parents. I didn't want them to worry about me or to be concerned about what I was getting up to on the other side of the world.

Time passed, and as it did, my expectations grew. Getting a snippet of information that could be validated weekly wasn't enough. I had been to the circle a few years now, and the strange terminology they were using was starting to get to me. A few days before, at the circle, we were asked to meditate. It was guided; the teacher asked us, with the faculty of our imagination, to go into an imaginary garden, and in that garden would be a bench. On that bench, we would either meet a guide or a relative, and there would be a gift for us. Being a gardener, I felt very qualified for this meditation!

I followed the teacher's voice and walked up the hill, through the gate and into the walled garden. I walked beside a stream, over a bridge and there before me was the bench set out in a glade. I could see something small on it, and as I drew close, I saw it was red. A ruby, perhaps? A satin cushion holding a priceless object? I drew closer, and there before me on the bench was a bright red tomato!

A few days later, at home, I got ready to go to work. I was mulling over in my mind if I should go back to the circle or whether to give it all up as a joke. I got in my car and set off to the garden where I would be working that day. The thoughts and doubts that had become more persistent of late swam in my head. "How could the circle be of any use?" "I'm a young man; I should be going out doing the usual things young men do, such as going to the pub or a club, and what about parties!"

I turned the corner and drove up the main road, my doubts continuing. "After all," I thought, "how could anyone in their right mind get a tomato in a meditation?"

Then, at that precise moment, right in the middle of that busy London road, it was exactly that. Sat on the tarmac was a tomato! Goodness knows how it got there, but there it was, a large tomato, slap bang in the middle of the road in front of me. So, with that, my doubts were erased. Because of a tomato... I continued with my studies!

Reading for Myself

Julie gave one-to-one readings, and after a few terms, I plucked up the courage to book one for myself. These were separate from her school, and I gingerly drove over to her home. Julie was a little formidable, and my classmates and I all put her on a pedestal.

Like with her classes, she read on different levels. Julie said that I had been a well-known architect in ancient Greek times! She even said some of the very buildings I was responsible for were still standing as ruins. Curiously, she said that I was mainly interested in the outside of buildings.

Now, this was strange, as when I had arrived in the UK I had spent all my free time going around country houses and gardens. Weirdly, I had no particular interest in the interiors but much more so in the facades. I would stand outside the front of the grand buildings and gaze at the facade. This all made sense.

The flip side of that was that she told me that during the time when I was in Greece, how you were supposed to look and act was quite regimented, and this meant that I might not accept people who did not fit my own mould. She meant that I may very well have carried that belief system from ancient Greece into my life here, in London, in the twentieth century.

Julie also told me that I appreciated the spirituality inherent in beautiful things. This would explain my interest in antiques, I suppose. Regarding emotions, she likened mine to a tap, a tap that was on full bore! She said it was too much for people and I should turn it down. I had just thought

I was passionate. I remember her also saying that I had cried so much in my life that I could have drowned in my own tears. Sook Magrook came to mind.

Julie told it as she saw it. Sensibly, she saw the by-product of doing the classes was self-development. We were asked to look at ourselves, and she would often say, "Observe yourself", and talk about "energy management." It was the old adage of peeling off the layers of an onion to reveal our truer nature. It was a way of learning to love ourselves, too, though I didn't realise it at the time.

I couldn't underestimate this as it was proven to me during one class. We were doing an exercise with colour and its relation to the chakras, the energy systems, and the centres in our bodies, which stem from Hindu and Buddhist beliefs. As I followed Julie's voice and held a colour over my throat, involuntarily in my mind's eye, black goo, like oil, spilled out from my throat. When the time came, and we had to go around the class one by one and relate our experience, Julie looked quite horrified when I mentioned the black oil. There was a shift, and healing was taking place. This centre was being unblocked.

Julie's other teachers also offered private readings at their homes. After a few years of development, I decided to have a reading with Penny. I had seen her around at Julie's college as she taught another class, but I had never met her, so one day, I called and made a booking. Shortly afterwards, I arrived at her home, and she sat me down for a reading.

"Now, would you like to give yourself a reading?" she asked, "Or shall I give you a reading?"

Now, that took me completely by surprise. I was fascinated by the idea.

"How about half and half," I said, hedging my bets.

She read first, and then it was my turn.

"I will hold your energy," Penny told me as I prepared to read for myself.

I opened myself up and spoke aloud what I was seeing and feeling. I was amazed that I was receiving anything at all. I saw Moses' mother setting

Moses adrift on the river, floating down, swaddled on a basket. I felt Moses' mother's pain as she let the basket go. I saw this so strongly, "it can't be in my mind," I thought. The story of Moses seemed to be a parable of how some of my life had gone. I carried on, and suddenly, a vision of a sword came into my mind. Everything that I saw I voiced aloud.

"What kind of sword?" Penny prompted.

"Well, it is very large and completely plain," I answered. It meant nothing to me; it just came in on its own; again, it was a strong vision, and it felt spirit-given. A couple of things I said Penny said, "No, that's your mind," to keep me on track. Moses was to feature again a few years later.

Dead Rellies!

I had now been in the circle for over four years. There was a new lady in the group who we jokingly called the 'Astral Queen.' The astral plane is the dimension where people go when they pass over, which spiritualists also call the Summerland.

My teacher very rarely did exercises where we would bring these two worlds together. She said we were expressing their opinions, which may be no different from when they were alive. This surprised me as I had thought that when one goes over to 'the other side,' one would become illumined. That one would see things from all perspectives, not just from the limited, blinkered one we do in our lives here on earth.

This particular lady, the Astral Queen, had previously learned in a circle where linking into that dimension was all that was done, and consequently, it had become her area of expertise. We all loved it if she would give us a reading in class, as a relative would come through, and a message would be given and received. I remember a great aunt whom I had adored coming through. I felt a great comfort, and it was fantastic to hear from her in this way.

An Introduction to Spiritualism

The Spiritual Association of Great Britain (SAGB) was located in Belgravia, probably the most upmarket area you could find anywhere in London. The building had been leased out by the Duke of Westminster, and it turned out that a spiritualist, Lord Dowding, had been friends with the then Duke and had secured a 99-year lease. Not a bad location to have your head office, normally reserved for embassies and the most affluent of society.

I was amazed by the place. One would go through a revolving door at 33 Belgrave Square to a reception room before ascending a grand staircase into a Robert Adam hall with Adam ceilings and fireplaces.

The SAGB has some old relics of their own, marble busts and fine oil paintings. The main hall was kitted out with rows of old cinema chairs that had been screwed into the parquet floor of what formerly was a double reception room!

At the end of the room facing the square, they had built a raised platform where a grand piano, a lectern and a few chairs stood for the mediums to give their demonstrations of clairvoyance.

Twice a day for just a few pounds entrance fee, a medium would give what they called a 'public demonstration of mediumship'. I would go as often as I could. As I worked in the area a fair amount, I could go to their afternoon 'demonstration', as they called it, or pass by on my way home for their evening 'demonstration'. I noticed that I always got a message despite the fact that not everybody who attended would get a message. I now know that as my energy was so open, it made it easier for mediums to connect to me. Here the mediums were communicating with people who had passed away. They would announce who they had there and give a message backing this up with evidential information. To me, it was like they were speaking to God sometimes, and I put these people on pedestals.

"This is what I want to do," I thought.

Julie didn't like her students doing other spiritually based endeavours outside of her classes. I could see her point as it could dissipate one's energy, but we were all so keen many of us chose to ignore her wishes and carry out these extra-curricular activities. In fact, some of us had become spiritual junkies! Saying that, though, every time I went to a mind, body, and spirit festival, within 10 minutes of stepping foot in the place, I would get a headache and have to leave as the energy of so many people was overwhelming.

In class one day, Julie looked at me with her steely gaze.

"Are you doing something elsewhere?" She asked.

"No," I answered honestly.

"Are you sure?"

"No, I'm not," I assured her, feeling like a naughty schoolboy. I realised that she was picking up me going to Belgrave Square to see the demonstrations. Without me even realising it, I was learning just by being there. So, actually, Julie was correct, as it all involved the same 'energy.' Another time, when I was house-sitting for six months on a property with extensive grounds overlooking the Thames, Julie asked me if I worked in a park. I told her that I didn't, which was the truth, but it was the same thing. She was picking up the park-like energy from the house, and nobody would think I was living in a house in the middle of such a large garden in London. The grounds were so extensive it really was like a park. So, energetically speaking, Julie was completely correct.

I had attended a spiritual healing course with Rupert, Julie's husband, at Insight & Intuition. I could feel the healing energy coming out of my hands, so I felt qualified in my own way to do it. I remember when, in the class, during an exercise that involved holding my hands out and stretching them out towards my partner for that day, there was a crack of electricity. Of course, it could simply have been static from the shoes I was wearing!

After some digging, I found a community centre that would allow me to give spiritual healing to anybody who wanted it. I went one evening a week. No money changed hands, so what harm could it do, I thought. I was doing it to help people, and to bring positive change into their lives.

One of my first 'customers' was a French guy. He came into the room I had set up for the sessions, and I sat him down. I would start the healing as I had been taught, with my hands on the person's shoulders, asking them to take three deep breaths. I had soft music playing in the background, and many people would drift off to sleep. When the person was settled, I would move my hands about their energy field, through the layers of energy, not touching the person again until the end, when I would place my hands back on their shoulders and give them a squeeze to indicate that we had finished.

This French guy sat there, and as I had my hands out in his energy, I suddenly felt the strong presence of a nun. Giving healing was just that, giving healing, not giving messages, so when it was over, I simply said, "There is a nun around you". He made no comment on that, thanked me for the healing, and left. The presence was so strong I felt like I could reach out and touch her. It was like linking into fine champagne.

A couple of years later, I bumped into this same chap while walking down Camden High Road.

"Hi there," he said, recognising me. I remembered him, and we exchanged a few words.

"Do you remember when you gave me healing and said there was a nun around me?"

"Yes," I replied, recalling the strength of the feeling.

"Well, I'm an orphan, and I was brought up by nuns in France", he said. "The main nun that brought me up, I hadn't seen her for years, and the day after you said I had a nun around me, I was contacted by the French embassy as she was trying to get in touch with me, as she had sensed that I wasn't well. Funnily enough, I had thought the nun had been in the spirit world, but now I realised I was picking up the beautiful thoughts that she had surrounded this person with. If you think of someone, it doesn't matter where they are; that thought will travel to their aura. This is one of the reasons that prayer is so important.

My mind was full of many prejudices, just as Julie had said in her reading about fitting the mould and for some reason, I thought that nuns were a miserable lot. Perhaps I had watched too many old black-and-white movies as I had no contact with any Catholics during my entire life. This nun that I had linked into couldn't have been more different from my preconceived notion of what nuns were like. As I alluded to earlier, it was like linking into the finest champagne, bubbly, light, and just incredible. Wherever I got my ideas about nuns from, they were proven to be as far from the truth as possible. I changed them immediately after accidentally linking into her beautiful energy.

Chapter Three

A PREDICTION

I sank into the sofa with my mug of tea and prepared myself to be treated to the reading, the one that had so mysteriously, so suddenly dropped onto my doormat that gloomy winter morning. I still couldn't believe that Anne could give me a reading so many months after I saw her, and remotely. What an extraordinary talent that was. Funnily enough, at that time, Julie was teaching us about reading from different levels, 'higher conscience,' she would call it, and this was a perfect example of that, whirring away in my cassette player.

Anne's soft, English accent filled the room. She touched on past lives. Apparently, I had been a drummer boy in a past life, fearlessly leading the troops into battle. A knight in armour was mentioned, but it was apparently far off and relevant to my future.

She talked of the night sky and how I could draw inspiration from it. A military regiment was mentioned and even a name that I was connected to in the regiment. As she changed levels, she said word for word, "At some point in your life, you will feel drawn to join a group of like-minded people to sing your note of blessing into the earth".

"Wow", I thought. Being a gardener, a great nature lover and someone who loved to sing, I couldn't think of anything nicer to do. I wasn't sure what it was to do such a thing but it sounded right up my street, to "sing your note" and if it was a blessing into the earth, all the better!

The reading went on, my tea cold, untouched and forgotten beside me. I felt incredibly special having all this information. I was simply amazed that this lady could record me a personalised reading months after meeting me. So much time had passed by that I had forgotten all about her promised reading.

Anne also talked about me knowing my place on the "planet", as she put it, and to know who I had been and who I would be. My mind boggled. My levels of self-esteem had fluctuated throughout my life, so I thought she was referring to that to give me a boost. She said that I had the opportunity for my mind to be "one pointed" and that I could link into the Akashic records, whatever they were! I had to look them up and discovered they are a place that holds all the information on your past, present, and future lives, as well as your destiny. It is a place where all truths are known, not just about ourselves, but for everyone who has been and will be.

I did not feel worthy to look upon such a place. Was it something that anyone could see or should see? Was I worthy of all this lofty talk? I stood up, hit the rewind button, and immediately listened to the tape again.

Past Life Workshop

My fellow classmates and I were no different from any other group of like-minded people with a common interest. We would compare notes and discuss anything and everything going on in the spiritual world. We were all now 'spiritual junkies', desperate to learn about or simply to discuss anything new related to our new shared passion. We were no different than football fans and twitchers, or to slightly misquote that Kinks song, dedicated followers of fashion. We were simply all in the boat of following. Julie was a follower of Madame Blavatsky from the Theosophical Society and would say it was all "Glamour."

A classmate had spoken highly about a past life regressionist she had seen, claiming that she was the best in her field. Jodie, a fellow classmate, and I decided to book a session. We went along together, using each other for mutual support. We were sitting in the waiting room, and neither of us knew what to expect. Jodie was called in first. An hour later, she returned, and it was my turn.

It was a bit like the reading with Penny in so much that things weren't served up on a plate. We were provided with a platform or the right conditions, and then our own experience told us what our past lives had been.

I was instructed to lay on a comfortable reclining chair before being given a guided visualisation to follow. I guess it was a form of hypnosis as I was guided to walk down ten steps after being put in a relaxed state. At the bottom of this stairway, there was a corridor with closed doors running off it. Jodie and I were asked to go through the various doorways and describe aloud what we saw.

Behind one doorway, I was in a desert, living the nomad's life. Another doorway I didn't want to go through, not a nice life that I didn't want to remember. Through a third door, there was a loud, jolly man, full of magic. I thought he was a guide rather than a past life, and it felt very real meeting him and left a lasting impression on me. Jodie waited for me afterwards. We didn't share our experiences as they seemed very personal and private for both of us.

Curiously, years later, I was at Janet's, another medium, for a weekend day workshop she held every month. That weekend, she had invited the medium Janet Mckensie, who also used to do past life regression. When my turn came around, I remember the floor became sticky underfoot. When I relayed this, I was told that it was blood on the floor. Janet said I had been in a war and that it had been a life that I had not liked very much at all.

I remembered the door I wouldn't go through in my previous experience of past life regression. Some things are left best not known. What purpose would it serve me to relive some violent, traumatic event or life from deep in my past? I have never seen the point of violence and didn't want to have some horrible memory brought back and thrust upon me now. I have always preferred to concentrate on the better things in life, believing that God wanted this to be a planet of joy.

In one of Julie's readings, she said I had asked the spirit world to be a medium. They had heard my request, and it had been granted as it was a genuine one undertaken with the right motive. But she added that I had been very brave as I had not realised what I would need to go through in order to achieve it. Very much a double-edged sword. One has to work through any dross, clutter, and conflict in one's life and observe oneself lovingly to become a clear channel and be able to work for spirit and do good.

Julie would say that someone working at a supermarket checkout could be giving more spirit healing to people buying their weekly groceries than a qualified healer. I knew what she meant. Papers and certificates are not always relevant. When two people are bonded through the link of love, a licence is just a formality; they are still married in the eyes of spirit. If a potter can turn clay, is a certificate necessary? The person can still throw a pot. I know a sculptress who went to university to obtain the qualification. This does not necessarily mean they are artistic. In spirit, the qualification is not the measure of a person's skill, ability, or worth. It is our way of being that matters, whether you are aware of it or not. We are all channels of energy and spirit. We wouldn't be alive if we didn't have a spiritual counterpart!

An Irish Ghost Story

Whilst on holiday in Santorini, I met a girl called Sarah. We got on well, seemed to enjoy each other's company, and, to cut a long story short, we agreed to go on holiday together to Ireland. Although we hadn't discussed it openly, I think we both knew it was a holiday to see if our relationship would go anywhere, so as I packed for the trip, the last thing on my mind was spiritual matters! In fact, I was glad to have a complete break from that side of my life, which had become all-encompassing, and to go away with someone who had absolutely nothing to do with that sort of thing.

It was Valentine's Day weekend, but foolishly and somewhat naively, we had not booked any accommodation. We arrived at our chosen corner of the Emerald Isle only to discover every guesthouse, hotel and bed and breakfast was fully booked, the rooms all taken by couples with the same idea of a romantic weekend away, all of whom were considerably more organised than us!

We had planned to stay in Kilkenny but were forced to venture further and further out of the town, trying to find an empty room for the evening, and by the time the night drew in, we were in the countryside, many miles away from the town.

Eventually, we saw a lit-up building set off from the main road. It looked like a castellated manor house, and we decided to see if they had any room for us to stay. We drove up the gravel drive, pulling up in front of its grand exterior before walking up a flight of steps to the front door. I knocked on the heavy wooden door, and before too long, muffled footsteps could be heard before the door swung open to reveal a man wearing, of all things, a safari hat! Alas, this was also booked out, but the owner said they had vacancies the following evening should we wish to return. The rates were cheap, and as we both loved period properties, we decided to return the next night.

We eventually found somewhere to sleep that night, but it was so late by then, and we were so knackered by the very long day we both fell fast asleep as soon as we climbed into bed.

The following day we had planned to visit a waterfall we had heard was well worth a visit. As we drove over a bridge approaching the falls, I felt a mischievous nature spirit. It was subtle, and I couldn't decide if it really was a nature spirit or merely a trick of my mind. I had such an active imagination that I always double-checked myself. We arrived at the car park to find another car there, which made us feel easier about being there as the place felt very remote and the weather was closing in.

As we set off, walking along the track that would take us to the falls, a mist came in, and after a moment's deliberation, we decided to carry on despite seeing another couple coming back in the opposite direction, obviously returning to the safety, and dry, of their car. The mist became thicker and thicker as we drew nearer to our destination, climbing up beside the tiered falls. By the time we reached the top, we could barely see more than ten feet in any direction. We stood, getting our breath back, listening to the falling water drumming on the rocks below. Suddenly, a gust of wind took up, picking up the water from the falls now below, lifting it and throwing it back at us. We were wet through to the skin. It was as though somebody had thrown a bucket of water over us!

Sarah then panicked and was adamant she wanted to carry on walking over the moor rather than retracing our steps down the steep banks besides the waterfall and back to the car. I argued that we could be walking for hours and that it was best to carefully make our way back down the cliff. As we slowly climbed down, the mist had turned to fog and was now so thick we could barely see the ground in front of us. At one point, we came to a sheer drop, and I had to guide every step of Sarah's back down until we reached the relative safety of level ground before eventually finding our way back to the car, wet and weary.

Sarah had seemed to regress into a helpless maiden in distress during the experience, forcing me to do my best impression of a knight in shining armour. As I drove back over the bridge, I felt the nature spirit again. I felt that we were not welcome there. Knowing that if I'd have said anything about the strong sensations I was picking up, I would have freaked Sarah out, so I kept my thoughts to myself.

We returned to the grand house we had briefly visited the evening before, which we subsequently learnt had been a former rectory. We were hastily shown to our room, which was at the top of a grand staircase and along a corridor. Downstairs, there was a large reception room dominated by a burning log fire, which we were told we had free use of. With that, the proprietors announced they were going to mass, the reason for our hasty introduction into their home, and promptly left us to our own devices. It seemed odd that they would leave us there alone in their grand home without knowing us. The man was quite eccentric and again wore the safari hat which he had sported the previous night. I noticed he did leave it by the front door as he left for mass however!

I left Sarah in the drawing room in front of the fire and said I would go upstairs and hang our soaked clothes on the radiator to dry out after our waterfall experience. I went up the staircase along the corridor and into the room. As I was placing the clothes on the radiator, I suddenly heard a blood-curdling scream right outside the door. I opened the door, thinking it was Sarah playing a trick on me, only to find the corridor was completely empty. The hairs on the back of my neck stood up, and I became afraid. I rushed downstairs and burst into the drawing room to be greeted by the sight of Sarah calmly playing the piano. I was, for the second time in my life, properly scared. I stood by the fire, feeling that it was the safest place to be in its light and warmth.

"Did you hear anything?" I asked Sarah, keeping my voice as level as possible.

"No, why?"

Not wanting to scare my partner too much, especially after her reaction at the waterfall, I played down what had happened, deciding to wait until the owners returned.

An hour or so later, they came back, and keen to find answers to the questions whirring inside my head, I wasted no time interrogating them.

"Do you have a ghost here?" I boldly asked. "A little girl?" The scream I had heard was undoubtedly that of a small girl.

The couple glanced nervously at each other before the man, now bare-headed, answered me.

"We have only been here a year and have never seen a ghost," he began, "but the people in the village say there is a ghost here."

Then, together, they proceeded to tell me the story. About 100 years earlier, the then priest's daughter, who was 18 at the time, had drowned in a lake in the garden, a lake that had since been filled in. I realised that it wasn't a ghost I had heard, but the scream from when the unfortunate girl was drowning. Her name was Ophelia. Ophelia was not haunting the house, but that awful scream was somehow left in the atmosphere of the place, like a kind of recording, and I had linked into it accidentally.

When people go to spirit, it is a place of peace and healing. However, when bad things happen, and good things for that matter, it can leave an imprint, a little like a stuck record. The owners didn't seem overly pleased that I had mentioned the 'ghost,' but that didn't deter me from being very cheeky. I wrote in the visitors' book, "RIP Ophelia." It didn't seem irreverent to me as I knew her soul had moved on long ago.

The next day, we were driving along a country lane. As we made our way between the high hedges, I looked to my right and looked out through a farm gate. At the same moment, there was a cow. Our eyes met for a fleeting moment, but in that moment, I had the most extraordinary 'knowing', and I was (I can't think of a better way of putting this) 'downloaded with information'. I can't say that the cow spoke to me, but it certainly seemed like it. I was channelling from the cow's energy.

"We are leaving the planet," it 'told me.' "When we chose to serve man, it was not in the agreement that we would be treated so appallingly, so we are leaving. We shall go to a holding pen in the ether and await a new place that is ready for our energy."

When I returned to London, I told an Irish client what had happened. I told her so that I would have a witness. Six months later, foot and mouth broke out in the UK and Ireland, resulting in thousands of animals having to be slaughtered and burnt.

At the time, I thought it meant that all the cattle in the world would perish, but this was not the case. My client said she thought of what I had said as she saw the cattle being burnt in bulldozed piles in Ireland on her TV.

The romance did not blossom, and Sarah and I didn't see each other again!

Prediction Realised

About a year after receiving the taped reading from Anne, I was back cashing in on my door duty at the college, four stints as a doorman in return for a free workshop. This time, I opted for a yoga class. When I arrived, I was surprised to see that the teacher was a woman who I had stopped at the door a few weeks earlier, only for her to brush past me laughing, almost with a "Don't you know who I am?" attitude. I was a bit disappointed and didn't think I would get much out of the class.

We did various exercises and postures, all foreign to me, having not done any yoga before, and then we were asked to lie on the wooden floor. The teacher came around, making adjustments to people's bodies, straightening a limb here, relaxing a neck and shoulders there. When she came to me, she moved my hips just a little and then moved on. My whole body started to vibrate. It was as though I was in the middle of two opposite magnets. It was a very comfortable feeling, and I don't know how long it lasted. I 'came to', and the class was continuing around me.

"Wow, who is this lady?" I thought, putting aside my earlier disdain. At the end of the class, she announced that she was arranging a trip and that anybody should put their name down if they were interested in "singing their note of blessing into the earth." She said it like that, word for word, from my cassette reading from Anne. My heart leapt!

I made my way to the front. "A medium told me about this," I said as I put my name down on the sheet of A4, feeling very important. She raised her eyebrows but said nothing. The trip was to Pakistan before following the old silk route over an arm of the Himalayas and into the Tarim basin in China, finishing at a Buddhist monastery at a place called Flaming Mountain. This monastery was where the singing into the earth was to take place.

There were several group meetings before the trip. At one of the early ones, the yoga lady tore into me for having expectations about the trip, I think because I told her it was foretold. I resolved there and then not to even read the itinerary! How could I have any expectations if I didn't even know what we would be doing or where we were going? I may not have read the itinerary, but I left with a knowing that something very special was about to happen.

As I was new to the group, which was mainly made up of people who had travelled with this lady before, I felt that I was being vetted by her groupies to get my measure. This mild intimidation didn't bother me; I had nothing to hide or prove to anyone and would just be myself.

The route had been handed over to a travel agent who specialised in tailor-made holidays. Everything was expertly organised, and all we had to do was attend the evening sessions beforehand and turn up on the day of departure with our bags. At the last moment, I packed a red silk handkerchief into my bag, then set off to meet my travel companions. We numbered 24.

Chapter Four

THE QUEST

I had never been on a spiritual trip before. Everyone on it kept laughing at me when I said it was a "holiday". Being the sensitive, absorbent soul that I can be, I was prone to picking up other people's energies, so any kind of break was always a holiday for me after the pressure of my gardening business. My day job was relentless, and the clients could be demanding, so it is little wonder that it felt like a holiday.

I wasn't very good at taking breaks, and the city energy of London was wearing after too long a time there in one stint. I could fully understand how many people had weekend homes in the countryside. I had friends in Kent where I would sometimes spend the weekend. I would always come back feeling refreshed and optimistic, away from the city's grind, or as my mother called it when visiting, "the rat race"!

In truth, though, this was more like a quest. Most of these people had been on trips with this lady before, including to places such as Israel, Sinai, and Egypt. We flew into Islamabad and settled into a hotel for the night. The next day, we got into two minibuses and off we drove.

I couldn't believe how crowded Pakistan was. Even as we drove into the countryside, the roads were lined with shops and men. Being a Muslim country, there were never any women in sight except occasionally on the rooftop of their house, where they could be seen threshing that season's grain. We drove on and on, leaving the towns behind, towards the mountains that loomed ahead of us. Eventually, we met the Indus River, the two minibuses pulled over, and we all piled out.

We walked 100 yards through the rocks until we came to a large stone with a carving. The leader started to talk about the carving. I heard a voice in my head say very clearly, "There is a much better carving on the other side of this rock." This startled me! Where had this voice come from? Who did it belong to? I didn't have the courage to repeat what I had just heard, so I slowly edged myself to the side of the group and then walked around to the back of the rock. Sure enough, there was another carving! "Hmmm, strange," I thought. I kept the experience to myself.

We drove on for another day before stopping at another hotel for the night. The next day, as I awoke and lay in bed briefly, I heard a voice again, but this time, it was coming from just outside my ear!

"Find the point within your heart which is all loving, not the point which loves one minute and hates the next," it whispered to me. I got up, took a shower and had a quiet weep.

What beautiful and profound words, and what a tall order, too.

On and on, we drove. We stopped again at the Indus river, where a swing bridge spanned the fast-flowing torrent. As a group, we walked over the metal structure, but as we got halfway across, I realised I had left my wallet on the seat of the bus; well, at least it wasn't in my pocket. I excused myself and rushed back to the minibus, where, sure enough, the wallet was on the seat. I returned to the group, and the leader sounded a note as I approached. I felt like a prodigal son!

At one point, we stopped for a toilet break where those in need of relief could head for a rock big enough to hide their modesty. We were in the middle of nowhere and had been driving for hours. We all bundled out to stretch our legs and wandered around among the strewn rocks. I turned around, and standing before me was a short local chap dressed in a black tunic with his hands outstretched towards me. I had no idea where he had come from; he hadn't been there a moment earlier! He held up a piece of newspaper, and in the middle was a large quartz crystal. His clothes looked like silk. His hair was very greasy, and he looked like he may have had difficulty recalling his own name! I beckoned him to sit down and gave him a Pakistani note in exchange for the crystal. "Nangaperbert," he said, pointing to a snow-covered peak in the far-off distance. That was where the crystal had come from, a mountain peak high in the Himalayas.

Another in the group had witnessed what had happened and laughed, saying that the man had made a beeline for me. I thought it was all a part of a great synchronicity and that I was meant to have the crystal. Years later, as I pen this, I realise it was because I was wearing a wide-brimmed hat. The local man may have seen it as a sign of rank. Nevertheless, it was still synchronistic.

When we stopped that evening, the red silk handkerchief was hanging out of my bag, so I took it at once and wrapped the crystal in it. I couldn't sleep that night due to the energy emanating from the crystal, so for the rest of the trip, I packed it deep inside my bag. The leader had brought along a book of her poetry. One night, she read us a poem all about a crystal. Was it that crystal? I wondered to myself.

We drove on, past the remote towns of Gilgit and Gulmit and through the Hunza Valley, an area where the local people worship the Aga Khan as a God. It was an incredibly beautiful place, with the mountains towering above us on either side and the Indus River raging below us. The road we drove along had been carved out of the side of the mountains. We were driving up and up, getting higher and higher. One morning, I awoke from a dream of flying over a lake.

The leader announced at breakfast that we were going to have a picnic at a summer village. We turned off the Karakourum Highway and headed up a dirt track, driving as far as we could before walking the final stage to the picnic spot on foot. We were very spoilt with Sherpa-type people carrying everything for us. All we had to do was get ourselves there.

We arrived at the designated spot and laid out our things on a terrace. I looked around. We were surrounded by mountains. There were terraces for crops, a small village of low-built mud houses, and a lake at the bottom of the valley. To the far right and over a ridge was a glacier.

Jesus was here, I thought. I could feel him all around me. All day, I couldn't get it out of my head. Jesus had been here! I could feel his presence; it was tangible as if I could reach out and touch him. As I looked at the group having lunch, a strange idea came over me. What if some people on this trip had been around at that time, during another lifetime? How did I know what Jesus felt like? I didn't know, but he had been to these parts. I just knew it. I felt it.

We took a walk to the glacier, and as we walked past the lake to get to it, I spontaneously jumped in, and everyone followed. The water had sulphur in it, so we all floated, very much like the Dead Sea. I remembered my dream of flying over a lake.

At the glacier, we could hear it cracking and creaking eerily as it made its slow and relentless way down the valley. It was a strange day for me, and I returned to the coach, lost in thought.

That night, I had another dream, one that told me, "The seeding from Sirius was a mistake." I awoke none the wiser, as I was not into any spiritual mumbo jumbo as I saw it. I didn't know about the planets or their purported properties, but I did know that Sirius was a planet. "The seeding from Sirius was a mistake." Now, what did that mean?

We drove on and on, finally reaching the last settlement. The cows had made way for yaks, and the sheep had made way for goats as we started the ascent of the Karakorum Mountain pass. This had to be done very slowly so that none of us would get altitude sickness, which can be debilitating and even fatal. Up and up we climbed, but thankfully, we made the ascent without incident.

There is a no-mans-land between China and Pakistan, which neither country owns. It was so quiet. I felt a natural high from the altitude and I was so happy.

We had another picnic among the tundra-like vegetation. I was eating my lunch when I looked over and saw that one of the people from the group had changed into someone from history. But how is it I recognise him I thought? Had I been his right-hand man? Or was I a Native American Indian? I had no idea, but I felt this so strongly. I leaned over to the leader, who was lying down, and whispered into her ear.

"John Steven's was General Custer!"

She let out a peal of laughter. "I should think he probably was!" She said, still laying on the floor. Nothing more was said.

I lined the broken biscuits in my hand in order of size and started to eat them, one by one, from the smallest to the largest.

"Who will swap their fur coat for a biscuit?" I said, laughing. There had been a lot of starvation in this land. Clutching the last of my biscuit crumbs, we were ready to move on. I was high from the altitude, and my third eye was fully open. We bundled back into the bus. I rearranged the biscuit crumbs in descending order of size. The leader scoffed as she walked past, spotting the broken bits of biscuits in my palm. I had taken a book with me to read, The Horse Whisperer. I took the book out of my day bag, turned to the next page, and there were the words, General Custer!

I walked to the front of the bus and put the book in front of the leader.

"See," I said, putting my finger under the two words as if to back up what I had just seen and voiced. It was weird having all of these experiences without trying. It felt like that run of paranormal experiences I had all those years ago that had started my journey to this Himalayan high place.

We reached the Chinese border post. I was amazed at how the atmosphere could change so quickly. The terrain and the people were all so different. We were entering the land of the Tajik and Uyghur people. This country had not seen many westerners. A fellow traveller, Arthur, was very tall, and everyone stared at him. He must have seemed like a giant to them.

We crossed the border and drove on, staying that night at what used to be an old Russian embassy. I don't know what had gone on there, but it wasn't good, and there was a bad vibe, especially in the front foyer, which I felt every time we went in or out. That night, I dreamt three things. The first was that I would landscape gardens all over the world. The second was that my mother would find a companion in her old age, and the third was that when my father was very old and using a walking stick, he would come over and visit me. At the time, the idea of me landscaping internationally seemed very far-fetched. However, several years later, this dream came true when I received a commission in Italy, Spain, Bahrain, and Slovakia.

As this had come true, I thought my other two dreams would materialise. I felt it was God, the universe, talking to me. Sadly, this wasn't to be the case with my second and third dreams. A few years later, I told my mother the dream about her finding a companion. I think she thought that I was hinting at her rather than relaying a prediction. I hadn't told my family any of my experiences as I thought they would think I had become unstable! I didn't want my parents to worry about me, particularly living so far away. I hadn't come from a background where spiritual happenings were commonplace or even acknowledged, at least not that I knew of.

It was announced that the next day, we were going to 'the caves of the three immortals.' There was a myth that three Buddhists who had reached higher states of consciousness had lived there. Our leader also told us there was a myth that Mother Mary was buried there. Some miles before we reached the cave, I noticed a change in my mood. I started to weep a little. The closer we drove, the more I cried. After a bit, I was weeping non-stop.

The bus stopped, and we all got out. I felt drawn like a magnet to this place; wave upon wave of energy was coming from the caves. I looked up. In the distance, cut into a rock face halfway up a cliff with a river running along its base, were the three caves. The energy was divine, but it was sad. 'Divinely sad' if that could be said. If I had to put it into words, 'it was the divine aspect of the masculine without any divine feminine', so although divine and sacred, it was barren at the same time. Presumably, the divine feminine would feel the same as an equal opposite.

Weirdly, I also felt that I was at a funeral. I knew whose bones had been held in this place from times past. If that is the divine masculine, I wish I could experience the divine feminine. I knew there was no way that Mary was buried there, that was not her energy, no way. Perhaps three Buddhists had lived there, but that was not their legacy energy either. Bones had been there; I knew it was like I was at a funeral; the funeral was of Saint Peter. I had linked to his essence. I don't know how I knew; I just did! That night back at the old Russian embassy, I had a sleepless night. I knew there was something I was just not getting.

The next day, we had lunch in a dusty restaurant. I looked at everyone in the group. I thought of the Jesus vibe in the summer village. What if some people in the group had past lives in biblical times, I thought again. Before we got onto the bus, I spoke with someone in the group while we stood on the roadside. I looked into her eyes, and suddenly, they changed like a kaleidoscope. I was now looking directly into the eyes of Jesus. I clocked again that I had recognition. I didn't say anything. I was looking into the eyes of Jesus. We embraced. I asked myself, "How do I recognise these eyes?" It was like the General Custer experience, seemingly random but energetically very specific, as though I was meeting somebody from my past.

Well, over 20 years later, I was told a similar story. A friend I knew through the spiritualist church had lost her sister-in-law through old age. A month later, this friend was leaving a church service and turned to chat with the working medium. The medium's eyes changed and became those of her sister-in-law! It was her sister-in-law's way of coming through just as it had been here.

The next part of the journey took us into the Taklamakan Desert, which also goes under the charming names 'the desert of no return' and 'sea of death!' The terrain would be too hard going for the minibuses, so we transferred into several jeeps and an old truck that carried the tent and provisions across the sands. We were headed for a holy Buddhist stupa located near Rowak. The Buddhists said that a new energy would emerge from this place. That was all that I was told. How on earth the drivers found it in this featureless landscape of endless sand dunes, I will never know. It was before the days of satellite navigation, and all they had to rely on was a paper map. We drove on and on through the sand until the truck and jeeps eventually stopped, with no stupa yet in sight. We pitched the tents and rested for the remainder of the day, ready to set off on foot first thing in the morning.

The next morning, we were up bright and early and, in single-file procession, made our way across the sand dunes to our destination. The stupa rose up above the sand dunes, but at first, it was not easy to spot as it seemed to be made of mud the same colour as the dunes that stretched around us for hundreds and hundreds of miles. Around the stupa was what was left of its surrounding walls, with one end completely abandoned to the sand. The leader told us that we should do whatever we were drawn to do, and then she lay beside a bush and promptly went to sleep! I had a sense that she had a feeling of mission accomplished. She had been guided to take us all to this place and now that role was fulfilled. I walked around the stupa. The sand was up to the outer walls at one end, with it levelling out along the other side. The desert was doing its best to engulf it.

Robbers had been there at some time in its history, and one side of the stupa had been hacked and broken into. Whatever contents were at its heart had long been removed.

I felt drawn to one end. I sat a while facing the side of the stupa from the top of what once was the enclosing wall before getting up and walking down the sand bank to the stupa's base. I acknowledged the face and walked slowly anti-clockwise to the next side. As I approached 90 degrees, I turned and acknowledged its face. It was an honouring. This was the side which had been hacked into, revealing a hollow alcove. As I walked slowly on, each step became heavier. A feeling of shame came over me. I began to feel that I was walking back in time. I walked on to the third side, acknowledging and honouring it. The feelings of shame and of going back in time became stronger and stronger with each step, and as I walked to the fourth side, these feelings were even stronger. Still, I turned and faced the fourth side. I honoured it.

As I walked the last quarter back to the first side, going full circle, I hung my head in total despair and wailed. The shame bearing down upon me as I walked back in time was just too much to bear. As I neared full circle, the full extent of man's shame from the past two thousand years ran through my body. The full extent of humanity erring from its divine path washed through me. Humankind had not followed the spiritual path since the time of Jesus. They had not followed his teachings.

I acknowledged it all as it flowed through me at the foot of the final side, where I had started. It was only through acknowledging it all that I could renounce it; how could I surrender something unless I knew what I was surrendering? This is why I had to have the experience. I didn't know why this had to pass through me. I guessed I was the soul there at the right time in the right place. Whatever, God was using me as his instrument to ground the energy.

This feeling continued to pass through me, that shame, and I surrendered it into the earth. Exhausted, I fell to the floor. Then, a change occurred. I was filled with a new energy. I was filled with bliss; I felt a great wonderment. Revived, I went again to the top of the sand bank. I faced the flank of the stupa and sang two songs, of what notes I don't know. A song of honouring, and the third song I turned away to sing it 'around the earth'. This was the new energy, coming out in the only way I knew how. Then I flopped down again to the sand, exhausted again.

My body rolled down the sand bank like a rag doll, joy enveloping me all the way to the foot of the stupa. This time, I sat in a yoga posture directed towards the stupa. After a while, we were called to have lunch. Looking back now, I think I had a thousand watts run through a 100 watt instrument.

In our lunch box, we had tomatoes. I asked the lady next to me, "If I cut this tomato, will you rub it into my leg?" To my amazement, she said "Yes" without hesitation. Then I asked if she would do my other leg, "Yes", she said again. I found out later that this was standard practice in the hotter parts of Italy, where she happened to come from, something they did to help them cool down. I then broke the bread roll in two and walked around the stupa, offering bread to the others. I had no wine. I was walking on a fine line of spiritual madness.

On the way back to the tents, we formed a winding line along the ridge of a sand dune so that one wouldn't sink into the sand. It made the journey easier and conserved energy. Our Chinese guide, Angela, strayed off the dune. "China", I called out and pointed the path to her. Two older ladies sank to their knees in the loose sand when we had to change dunes. "Ah, the humble", I thought. "You're doing so well", I encouraged them. I was in a strange, delirious place!

When we arrived back at our camp, everyone went for a lie down in the main tent to rest. I walked off some distance to the toilet. As I returned to the tent, a sand tornado was approaching, and I realised it was heading straight for me. I looked back towards the tents, and the leader had come out to see where I was. I faced her, and a moment before the whirlwind enveloped me, I stretched out my arms, knowing full well how dramatic the scene would look from where she was standing. She looked around to see if anybody was witnessing it, then turned on her heels and returned to the tent. The whirlwind passed over me as I shut my eyes, being smarted by the flying sand as it swept over me and then enveloped the tent.

There, the leader demonstrated a yoga posture for power. I repeated the posture I had made at the stupa, something very different from the one being shown. We were then invited to talk about our experiences. I relayed mine as best I could in my still semi-delirious state.

"What will you do?" Arthur asked me when I had finished.

After a long pause, I searched my mind and said, "Plant trees".

The next few days, I slowly came back to feeling myself again. It was just in time as we reached our final destination, the Buddhist monastery at Flaming Mountain in the Tarim Basin. This was the second lowest point below sea level on the planet, and as such, there was an oppressive heat. The orange mountains that surrounded us formed a kind of cauldron. This was where we were to sing our note of blessing into the earth.

As we exited the bus and started walking towards the monastery, the wind was blowing dust off the orange hills. The leader hurried forward and stretched out her hands with the dust in the background. It reminded me of the film 'The Sound of Music', and I took a picture just at the right moment. I sent the photograph to the leader after the trip. It was a powerful picture, and she sent a copy to her following. My whirlwind experience was the inspiration!

There was a row of long-deserted ancient cells cut into the cliff face, and the leader took us into three of these. In the final cell, we were to sound a note in unison. I filled my lungs to their maximum, and we all sounded a long note three times. It was a job done for all in the group. It had been an amazing journey, truly a trip of a lifetime.

We piled back into the bus and journeyed onto the local capital, Urumqi, to get a flight back to Islamabad, where we would catch a plane straight back to London. In the hotel the night before the flight, I felt very strange. Later, people said that I didn't even look like me. I didn't feel like me either. I was very quiet, and I took things extremely slowly. Gradually, I came back to myself. I think that with all the profound experiences I had undergone, I had loosened my spirit from my body, though fortunately, the cords were still there. It is hard to put into words. I think just how many watts had been run through me on that journey. As I said, a trip of a lifetime. In a reading later, Julie Soskin said I had nearly burnt a hole in my energy. I think she was referring to this experience.

When I arrived back in London, I felt very different. I was in a state of bliss. By the end of the trip, I felt that I had found that point within my heart that was "all loving". I remember rolling on my back lawn in pure joy with the daisies answering me back! Just like the women in the circle had said all those years ago, the flowers were dancing with joy. Shortly after returning to the UK, I went to the local swimming pool. As a gentleman came through the door that led to the pool, the energy of the whole place lifted; such was his energy. People do not realise the energy that they carry!

Certain other things changed in my life at that time. For several months, I kept meeting people with the name of Peter or Simon. I was also offered to join yoga classes that the leader of the trip to the Himalayas held.

"You aren't a cult, are you?" I asked gingerly, half joking.

"Oh, we are far too irreverent for that!" she laughed.

Next Steps

I couldn't decide whether or not to meet a holy woman, Amma, who was going to be at Battersea town hall. Amma was a highly regarded Indian mystic who toured Europe teaching. People would line up for hours just to get a hug from her. Anyway, the matter was decided in a way that previously would have amazed me, but now, it almost seemed run of the mill. Her thoughts entered my mind, telling me I didn't need to go and see her. It was telepathy. My psychic ability really had shot through the roof after my trip.

Back at Julie's class one day, we had opened up, and Julie asked if anybody wanted to give a reading. I volunteered and channelled a reading through. I didn't have to think about it; it came through word for word from start to finish. There was somebody who was still grieving over the passing of a loved one. This person was punishing themselves and holding on to the deceased with their thoughts. It was the person's father.

"You are keeping me here," he said. "I have a fabulous future! Let me go!"

His soul needed to move on. This was the first time I heard from a spirit making a request to the earthly person, and it was not to be the last. This person had been a Daddy's girl, and so when Dad had passed, it was only natural for the person to hang on to her father with her thoughts. This kept him in a fixed place in the spirit world, and as he said, his soul needed to move on.

That wasn't the end of the reading, though. It also mentioned that places with spires attract spiritual energy, and we should make the most of any time spent in such places. Julie said afterwards that I had a saint with me. I knew that the essence of Saint Peter was still in my energy. It was a very profound reading. After the Taklamakan experience, I had become a very good channel. On that journey, I had rubbed shoulders with the best.

The following week, I was there early with one of my classmates, and we waited on the balcony, overlooking the glassed-in room which served as our classroom. Julie was in there giving someone a reading. "I like what she does, but I wouldn't want to spend half of my life with my eyes closed," I remarked. The following week in class, Julie was discussing her life and said, "I like what I do, but I don't like having my eyes closed for half of my life!" You should have seen the look my classmate shot me.

I continued the classes at Julie's for a while, but I felt I had learnt everything I could. It was time to move on. I had treasured those classes, and they had become a huge part of my life. I had gone every week for seven years and had loved every minute. Julie was a real gem. There is a saying that goes, 'When the student is ready, the teacher will appear.' That was exactly what had happened with me and Julie. The fruit was now ripe, and it was time for me to move on.

Meanwhile, my 'other life' carried on. I spent it largely trying to build up my gardening business and balancing that with attempting to have a normal social life. A good year must have passed with me not doing anything spiritual apart from going to the occasional demonstration at Belgrave Square for a few pounds.

I plucked up the courage to suggest to a friend that he accompany me to the SAGB. I wasn't trying to convert him, but I thought he might get something out of it for himself. We bought our tickets at the front desk and ventured up to the Adam hall. Many mediums served the SAGB, and they had an area blocked off from the public where mediums could stay over if they were visiting from outside London. Many of the mediums were fine, but the quality sometimes dipped!

On this particular day, a lady stood up to do a demonstration. She was linking to someone in the congregation and suddenly said, "Oh, there is a little dog with you. Now it is running up the aisle, here in this room." My friend was desperately suppressing fits of laughter. Sadly, this woman didn't give any evidence that anybody could relate to, and it was all quite wishy-washy. Walking back down the grand staircase, my friend could not hold back any more, and he laughed all the way out of the building! I was so embarrassed. I realised it wasn't for everyone, and after that, I kept my other life to myself. Mediumship done badly is an embarrassment, and as it is working with the unseen and with no script, it is something that is easily ridiculed.

After work one evening, I stopped for half a pint at a pub that happened to be near the SAGB. Standing at the bar, I was approached by a man. He introduced himself and said, "You go to Belgrave Square, don't you?" He recognised me from my visits to the demonstrations. "You should be in a class," he told me. It turned out that he was a working medium there.

"Join Sharry Clarke's class", he had said. That was my second lead. I wasn't looking for it, but life seemed so empty after my years at 'Insight and Intuition.'

Years later, I remember this same guy saying that a plane would come down and land on the River Thames. A while after that, a plane did come down and was forced to land on the Hudson River. Like with Julie, the energy was the same, and what he saw was correct; it just wasn't on the Thames; it was the Hudson.

So, my second phase of development started. This time, it was all about dead rellies!

Chapter Five

A SPIRITUAL BANNER

I took the working medium's advice and joined the Spiritualist Association of Great Britain! This centre was very different from the ones I had been to before. This came under the spiritualist banner and had an old-fashioned Victorian atmosphere about it. It was all about deceased relatives or 'dead rellies' as I called them. What excited me about this, apart from the fact that you were linking to the other side of life, was that it was very much about fact. We had to bring through information that could be proven. Of course, it was much deeper than that, as it was all about healing on one level or another and about helping people. It also wasn't just deceased relatives who came through, but anybody known or linked to the person, be it a childhood friend or a neighbour. It could be anybody. Linked through love, pets sometimes came through too.

Sharry was brilliant. We would be given time to open up spiritually in our own way after she gave the opening prayer. She would then ask who she felt drawn to that they might stand up and deliver a message whilst the others awaited their turn or sat in support. Often, someone would come in as a guest so we could tune into them as 'guinea pigs' so that we weren't just reading the same class members each week. We would then do at least one other exercise or guided visualisation in each class. Sharry did not say that you had to work this way or that way, but the group held the space, and the reader had a safe environment to work in.

At this time, when I went to sleep at night, I would often shut my eyes and see faces. They never said anything to me; I just saw the face. Repeatedly, I would see the face of a young Mary of Teck. She was a minor royal born in the middle of the 1800s and went on to marry King George V. After a time, I stopped seeing her face. I thought that she must have been a spiritual person when she was alive, and now that she was in the spirit world, she was helping newcomers develop. I didn't recognise the other faces, and Mary of Teck was the only one who came repeatedly.

Sharry was always reminding us to close down and said that we should consciously close ourselves down several times a day. It was very important to stay grounded and protected. I believe it is not from the dead who we need to protect ourselves from but from the living. The spirit world is a place of love.

I went every week to class, and it quickly became the highlight of my week, just as Julie's class had done so. Sharry and her class members would go to a local pub afterwards for a drink and a bite to eat. It wasn't long before I knew all the students and teachers there, and it became a social outlet.

After a second year, I joined another class, so I was doing two classes each week and weekend workshops three or four times a year. Now that I am a teacher, all these years later, I occasionally meet people who are as enthusiastic as I was. Each teacher had their way of working, but the constant for me was to practise, practise, and open up and close down, open up and close down, open up and close down. Sharry drummed this into us.

The SAGB held two weekend workshops a year at a hotel in Eastbourne. Here, you would be put in a class with a seasoned medium. Most times, I was in the esteemed Scottish medium Mary Armour's class. Mary was an old-school medium. For students, she would have 'Mary's 10 points to a message' that she suggested we follow. For a complete beginner, this was a perfect starting point. It put a structure to spirituality.

Linking to the loved one in spirit, the first five points were:

Was it a man or a woman?

What was their relationship with the sitter?

How did they die?

What was their job?

Where did they live?

And so on until ten, which was:

Why have they come?

As with all the teachings, this was an excellent guide, but after a while, one's own guides and working style would kick in. I loved my time with Mary and can still hear her thick Scottish accent now.

One evening in Sharry's class, we were sitting in meditation, and the energy of a tiger came into the room. The tiger's spiritual energy carried a great power with it, something beyond physical strength. I didn't see the tiger but felt him to such a heightened degree that it was almost physical. It is hard to describe. It sounds like imaginings, but it was so much more than a fanciful mind, though I have been guilty of that too! I had become like those other students all those years ago, who I thought were a bit weird speaking in this strange way and of strange things. "I have a tiger with me!"

As time passed, my spiritual muscles grew stronger, and I could give longer and longer messages.

The Mystic Piano

There was another teacher working at the SAGB who used to go on weekend workshops in Wales. I used to love these weekends away, too. They were held in a country house hotel on Anglesey. A wealthy Swiss lady had lost her daughter, and a medium had brought her daughter through. This had given the lady so much comfort that she bought a hotel in Wales, where the medium was from, and opened a spiritual centre there, which ran alongside the hotel business. The medium who brought her daughter through ran the spiritual centre while her husband ran the hotel. One day, we were sitting outside to do our exercises as the weather was so lovely, which was unusual for Wales! We had to close our eyes and link to the spirit world. I faithfully followed the teacher's directions.

Faintly, I could hear the spirit people playing the piano! I was very excited as hearing something from spirit was very rare for me. After the exercise, we had to share what we had got. When I told the group that I had heard a beautiful piano melody, I received a strange look from the group leader, and he moved on to the next person. That was not the adulation I had expected for Claireaudience! I had been told that the Swiss lady was staying at the hotel, and the next day, I was in the foyer and saw her coming downstairs holding some papers in her hand. It turned out they were sheet music. "I've just had a music lesson", I overheard her say." I nearly died of embarrassment as I realised it was her playing the piano the day before, with the window open upstairs! I cringed. It must have been clairpiano!

The Sinai Wolf

After my trip of a lifetime to Pakistan and China, I went on all the journeys that I could that the yoga teacher organised. To mark the turn of the century, a trip had been arranged to Mount Sinai to watch the sunrise from the top of the famous mountain for the new millennium.

We got a coach across mainland Egypt to the Sinai Peninsula. On arrival, we changed transport and then roughed it in four-wheel drive jeeps, travelling through the red valleys of sand. We wove our way through the valleys and gullies running through the hundreds of mountains that towered over us, going the 'back route'. We came upon a Bedouin family encampment where the valley had widened enough to support a little scrub. I didn't see it, but a well must have been nearby. Nothing much seemed to have changed with them for a few thousand years. Their large brown woollen tent was their nomad home. They tended their goats and a few sheep and grew a little grain in a wired-off pen. They were raising a clutch of chickens behind another scrap of wire. The Bedouin women were fully covered, and the two children were shy and wary. We must have seemed like aliens to them. We camped there that night, all choosing our own patch in sleeping bags under the star-filled night. I liked the emptiness of the desert.

The next day, we arrived at the foot of Mount Sinai and camped by a ridge, one ridge away from the mountain. It had been arranged that we pitch our tents within the old stone walls enclosing an orchard. I would never have called it an orchard myself, with the trees looking more dead than alive in the barren landscape and the four low stone walls falling apart in places. There was a well covered with a piece of battered corrugated iron, with a large stone placed on top to stop it from being blown away in the wind. With camp set up within the stone walls, we had a few hours of free time before the evening meal.

I checked my intuition. "Where do I feel like going?" I felt drawn away from the famous mountain whose outline could be seen rearing up over the ridge. Instead, I was drawn in the opposite direction. I assumed that I would be drawn to the holy mountain, of course. I set off, leaving the others, and in a moment, stepping over the crumbling wall, I was alone. A broad, low valley stretched out before me with dusty, low hills on each side. I sent out a thought to God. "I revere you, but you take me in the other direction!"

I headed down into the valley. Before long, I came across a farm. A simple, breeze-block house stood with grubby children looking out from the doorway to the accompaniment of dogs barking frantically, straining at their chains. It must be their orchard, I thought. Litter was strewn about the place. I walked on and followed the valley, which was gradually narrowing, the hills coming in closer and closer on either side until it was no longer a valley but a canyon. It was like something out of an old Western film. Now, the hillsides were small cliffs and, at times, at most 10 feet apart.

It wound around, and as I turned a bend, I saw that the canyon ahead was blocked by a rock fall. I climbed up and gasped as I got to the top. In front of me was an oasis, complete with palm trees. It was like something out of a film again, a desert oasis!

I walked forward into the opening. At the foot of a palm was a hole with freshly dug sand. I sniffed. A wolf. A she-wolf. She has cubs; I could smell them. How could I smell it when I had never seen a wolf, let alone smelt one? I didn't doubt for an instant what my brain was telling me, however. The information was clear. I moved on. Something caught my eye in the middle of the clearing. I moved forward. There was a small triangular piece of pink stone, different from all the stones around it. It was placed on a rock and had a bit of a tartan rag tied around it. I picked it up and put it in my pocket. All was still and quiet. A lot of arguing has taken place here I thought. I was in a special place, an oasis in the desert! A well was all that was missing. I rested a moment and made my way back, aware of the time I had been away.

The next day, we got up while it was still dark and made our way up the mountain to watch the sunrise on the first day of the year 2000.

After our sojourn in the Sinai peninsula, we returned to the capital and, after arriving in Cairo, went immediately to the pyramids. First on the itinerary was The Great Pyramid. We went into the centre of it, climbing up the narrow passages into the primary, dimly lit chamber. I didn't like it much in there. The air was stale and stuffy, and the atmosphere stifling. I kept myself to myself. Next, we went into the Pyramid of Cheops. This had an entirely different atmosphere, and for whatever reason, I felt a strong healing vibe.

We then went to look at the Sphinx. Unknown to me, beside the Sphinx is a temple ruin sunken into the desert. As a group, we ventured into it. A penny dropped. I pulled the stone out of my pocket, still wrapped in its rag. It was the very same stone that the temple was built out of. I half expected to see a niche in the rock that my arrow-headed shape would fit into! I had been watching too many Hollywood movies! There was another tourist group in the temple ruin, and they had a guide explaining the history. I went up to her.

"Excuse me, I said, where is the temple stone from?"

"Aswan," she replied.

A Christmas Gift

In the second class I started attending, in the last class of the year, the teacher gave us a guided visualisation, and we were told we would again receive a gift from the spirit world. My first thought was, not another tomato! We were asked to close our eyes and were guided through a visualisation of a garden. This was a favourite visualisation with many mediums. We were led here and there through a garden, the destination again being a bench. It was suggested that we sit down on this bench, and then we would be met by a spirit guide or a passed loved one, who would give us a present. As with all visualised meditations, nothing was forced, and there was no right or wrong. If we didn't see a guide or loved one, that was fine. It was down to our imagination, influenced by spirit, as to what state the garden was in.

Afterwards, we went around the class one by one, and we were invited to tell everybody what our Christmas gift had been. People were given gifts such as shimmering crystals, bright rainbows, protective cloaks, a new guide dressed in glorious colours and other wonderful things. When asked to share my gift, I said I had seen a plastic cube puzzle with ball bearings inside. My teacher asked what this represented to me.

"Balance and care," I said, as the ball bearings were difficult to get in the holes, and once they were in, they had to be held at a certain angle. That was the only symbolic message I could come up with.

About ten days later, I was due to work as a guest student with the medium Phylis Birdview. The teacher from the class was also there as he was going out with another of the students who was working that night, as we were joint guest students, or fledglings, as we were called. We arrived and passed by the raffle table with prizes on view. Straight away, I saw that one of the prizes was a pair of plastic cube puzzles with ball bearings. I did a double-take before pointing it out to the teacher.

"I am going to win those," I announced with complete certainty and went off to purchase a ticket. It was exactly what I had seen as my present from the spirit people in the garden.

We students started off the service with one message each, and then Phylis took over for the rest of the evening, and it all went very well. It was typical for a clairvoyant evening to finish with a raffle, tea, coffee and cakes. The bag of tickets was put in front of me so I could pick the first ticket. I put my hand in the bag and felt a ticket. "It isn't that one," I thought, letting it go and feeling for another. Phylis said, "He is going to pick his own ticket!" Settling on one, I pulled out my hand from the bag and displayed the number on the slip of paper. Number 74. Everyone roared. It was my Christmas present from spirit. I was so glad that my teacher was there so he could witness what happened, as I had told him of the puzzle ten days earlier as my Christmas gift in the last class of the year. I collected the prize.

Chapter Six

PLACE YOUR BETS!

I was invited to the dog races in the East End with my friend Sianne and her boyfriend. The night before, I dreamed about a dog and heard the word 'blue'. At the stadium that evening, I scoured the programme for a dog called 'Blue', and there it was, staring up at me out of the programme, Bluestone Boy. I hurried off to the betting kiosk and put down a fifty-pound note, convinced I would have a great win with my 'inside information.' The dogs set off, but things failed to turn out as I had hoped. The dog ended up coming in last!

I learnt a lesson that evening. This work is about helping people, not about self-gain. If it were for self-gain, the spirit people would give us the lottery numbers! That is not what it is about at all. It is not necessarily there to make our lives easier either. However, a greater understanding of life can make any bumps in the road smoother, both spiritually and in the physical world.

Another time, I was walking with the same friend on Hampstead Heath chatting. The conversation came around to Alsatian dogs.

"Isn't it funny how most Alsatian dogs are called Sheba?" I said.

"No, they're not," my friend replied indignantly, as though I was talking rubbish.

A second later, a loud shout of "Sheba" rang out over the heath, and an Alsatian bounded over the hill. That was a case of spirit backing me up, or, as a sceptic would undoubtedly say, simply a coincidence!

Chairing, the Next Step

The SAGB, like spiritual churches, held Sunday services. They were always looking for people to chair the services. I volunteered. This came with some responsibilities. We had to show the visiting medium to the medium's room, take a carafe and glasses of water to the lectern, ask the medium if they wanted any particular hymns, choose the reading, arrange who would pass the collection plate around, adjust the curtains as required and pull all of the hymn books out of the wooden chest by the entrance doors. Then, I would collect the medium at the right time, and we would wait outside the hall for the right moment to make a 'promenade' through the audience and onto the platform to the tune of the pianist's melody. In my early days, I was so nervous chairing the services, standing there facing people. As the months went on, this slowly wore off. Looking back, it was a great experience of working in front of people. Chairing was working with a script, whereas mediumship was not.

When the time came to work for spirit, I was already used to standing there. This wasn't a point I appreciated at the time, with my knees knocking! It took me a long time for my nerves to subside when public speaking. I found the lectern a comfort to hide behind!

After more years and years of being in a circle, I started to feel like the 'forever student.' I still loved every minute of it, but I knew again that it was time to move on. Students had come and gone, come and gone, and I was still there!

After a time, I was put in a 'finishing' class. The medium would get us to work as quickly as possible and also know whom we were going to, something that I didn't always do. There wasn't anything wrong with that, as I would ask spirit for information that would then take me to the right person. I remember years later, spirit started off a service's clairvoyance with "I'm with the person who drank a glass of pineapple juice this morning." A lady put her hand up to that! It was always exciting to see what spirit would open up with. Another time, it was, "I'm with the person who has ridden an elephant!" You never knew what would come next. With the elephant, apparently, they used to have elephant rides at London Zoo!

A treat about being in circle was always getting a message oneself. When I hadn't been in the UK for long, I advertised in a magazine as a Man Friday at a country house. I had an answer from a home in Kent and was asked if I would look after a child: a nanny, or manny as it is called! I went down and met the couple. Afterwards, they said, very nicely, it wasn't appropriate. Of course, they were right, as I had no mannying experience. Later, they called and said that as there was always a lot to do there, I could come and do other chores if I wished. I was delighted and did three day's work a week in exchange for free lodgings. I could not have stayed with nicer people. It was a great change from Australian life, and I fulfilled my ambition to live in a country home.

After seven months, I went to London for the garden centre job, but kept in touch with the family. When I left for London, Kate, the lady of the house, gave me a fork, knife and spoon, along with a bowl and plate. I treasured the blue Spode plate as it was a reminder of her and my time there. Tragically, seven years later, Kate got breast cancer and eventually succumbed to the disease, leaving behind three young children and a husband.

There was one girl in the class who would mention Kate to me from time to time, from spirit side. As I was so fond of her, this was a great source of comfort. Also, I didn't know anyone else who had passed at this time apart from my cousin Cherie and an old schoolmate who I had heard died tragically in an accident.

As Sharry wasn't a working medium at services, she could not take me out with her. When a student was ready, the teacher would often take the student to various churches to deliver the first or second message.

Mediums Phylis and Angela did this a couple of times with me, and I really appreciated it. Another medium, Alan would sometimes ask students to get up and work during his sessions at the SAGB.

Stars in Their Eyes

The SAGB medium, Angela, asked me to work at her centre in Milton Keynes. I was suffering from a nasty cold at the time, and as I travelled up, I felt pretty rotten. Halfway up the motorway, I felt so sick I nearly turned around. "I can't let Angela or spirit down." I thought, so I drove on.

I arrived to find that Angela had made shepherd's pie, but I was feeling so sick that I could only pick at it, eating the carrots and nothing else. I had brought a change of clothes, having come straight from work, so I went into her bathroom and took a few minutes to change. As I put my clean clothes on, I began to feel better and better, and when I emerged from the bathroom, Angela's mouth dropped open.

"Look at you," she said. It was like that TV show 'Stars in Their Eyes,' where the people are transformed in minutes. I felt like a new person; spirit had taken the sickness away! I had heard about this before: mediums whose sickness is taken away while they work for spirit, and when they finish, it returns.

"I feel it is going to be a special evening tonight," I told Angela as we rolled up at the healing centre. As it happened, only four people turned up to the demonstration, but it was fabulous. The energy that came through was so amazing that Angela went into a trance and gave the healing centre's owner some valuable information. Afterwards, the sickness did not come back. For me, this was nothing short of a miracle.

Open Platform, Further Steps

A monthly spiritual publication called 'The Two Worlds' was always for sale at the front desk of the SAGB. Most of the spiritual churches around London advertised their programme in the back pages. Most churches had a monthly evening called 'open platform.' This was where anybody could come along and have an opportunity to get up on the platform and deliver a message. It was aimed at fledglings who were preparing themselves ready to work.

I would circle all of the open platforms with a pen and write them in my diary. There would be a couple of these ink marks in my diary each week, representing different spiritual churches all across London. It was great practice.

After some months of attending these platforms, I kept seeing the same lady who, like me, felt she was ready to work. She had exactly the same idea and had sat in a circle in Pembridge Place. We struck up a friendship, and as she didn't drive, it wasn't long before I was collecting her at the train station, and we would go off to the various platforms together. Her name was Esi, and she was a psychic artist who would draw the person who was linking in and simultaneously give off a description and message!

It was my turn to demonstrate my link to the spirit world at one such open platform. I immediately felt drawn to a lady in the congregation.

"I am with you," I said, whereupon I started to give a very lengthy description of a lady in a bustle! I described her build, height, and facial features. I didn't normally go to such lengths or divulge such details, but the spirit person told and showed me, so I simply repeated it. The spirit person finished by saying that the person's name was 'Bessie.'

"My goodness," the lady exclaimed. "I was thumbing through an old family photo album, and there was a picture missing, but beneath where the picture would be was a name written: Bessie. I had wondered what she looked like, and you have just described her," she continued.

Another good piece of evidence was a lady in spirit who said the woman in the audience only had one plate left from a whole dinner service. "No," the woman said, "I have a dinner service in a cabinet." Spirit had told me so clearly, so I insisted. "Oh yes," she said, after a moment's thought. "I do have one plate from a dinner service. The house was bombed in the war, and everything smashed in the service except for one plate. I still have it." More great evidence. Another man came through and said that he had died with his boots on!

Being a young regular guy, I often wondered why I had now found myself talking about death all the time! It didn't seem right. Spirit would give you their ailments, how they had passed and sometimes their final memories. It is not that they remember them, but if it is our last memories of them, it is our way of remembering who they are. Spirits like to be remembered as fit, well, and at their best. Talking like this was morbid, and fortunately, as time passed, spirit spoke about many other things, only bringing through their way of passing if it was relevant.

First Demonstration, a Debut

Around this time, the medium, Alan from the SAGB, started to let the odd student get up and deliver a message during his demonstration. In the 'finishing school' class for mediums, I made many friends and got to know a girl called Carol. Carol also chaired for occasional Sundays, so there were times when I chaired for her and times when she chaired for me. We formed a good bond and worked well together. Alan mentioned that he may arrange a church for us to serve. Shortly after, it was agreed that Carol, a friend of hers and I had our first booking for a whole evening of clairvoyance.

This was my debut! All of the years of training and practise, this was what it had been building up to. I was very nervous as the day approached. The night before the event, I had a phone call. Carol and her friend had pulled out! My nerves doubled. After everything I had been through, this was my big chance, and I was determined not to let the opportunity slip through my fingers. I thought on my feet and called Esi, and she jumped at the chance. Like me, she was itching to work and, as far as I knew, had been a "forever student" too. I arranged to collect her, giving us plenty of time to get there. We were both so excited to have a lucky break at last.

As we pulled up in front of a large Jacobean mansion that had formerly served as a grand country house, our nerves started to kick in. We met the woman running the centre, a very severe lady who was being pushed around in a wheelchair. The mansion was now owned by the council and was turned over for a variety of community uses. This lady rented the period hall for spiritual evenings every month. Fortunately, she didn't know that neither of us had ever taken a whole service before, let alone an evening of clairvoyance! She led us down the corridor, effing and blinding coarsely, something we hadn't been expecting! We were ushered into a quiet room just off the hall. So much for all that chairing calming me down. I felt sick with nerves, and Esi was the same. The time for us to start arrived.

We stepped out into the hall and were met by an ocean of faces! The hall was packed to capacity. Esi set up her easel. We commenced. To be honest, a lot of it is a blur. From memory, the first connection was not accepted. The second connection was a diamond connection, and the information flowed with a lot of very specific evidence. This caught everybody's attention. The next was hit and miss, a weak connection, and it didn't do spiritual work any justice. The rest is just a nervous blur!

When it was all over, the organiser was wheeled over to us. "Well, at least nobody walked out," she said.

I decided to take that as a compliment. We drove back to the other side of London, stopping at a pub along the way for a small celebratory drink. Even though it could have gone better, it certainly could have gone worse. That night meant a lot to both of us, and we were now officially 'on the circuit'. I had made my debut and cut my teeth!

To begin with, Esi and I worked together. We rang around a few churches and spiritual centres and soon had plenty of bookings. I would link in and give the message, and Esi would draw and give off information.

It worked very well. We must have done this for two years before we felt that we would like to work for spirit in our own separate ways.

Another medium at SAGB was Paul Ronalds. He would often get humorous 'false teeth' messages. I thought this was brilliant, and sometimes spirit followed suit with me. To start with, I would just get that there was a funny incident with a particular family member that involved false teeth, and I would invite the sitter to tell the rest of the congregation what had gone on.

We heard stories, such as someone giving a speech in public when their teeth fell out on the floor, the person dutifully picking them up, putting them back on and continuing with the speech. Or when a chap was sick into the toilet bowl only for his teeth to follow. Another was how a lady was in the hospital, and the other patients all had false teeth as well; all the sets got mixed up, and the nurses didn't know whose were whose. Or how, at a dinner party, a chap coughed, and his teeth plopped into his bowl of soup. These stories always brought laughter. Eventually, I started to get the stories myself from spirit. Often, it all became so serious, with all that talk of dying, that it was good to have a balance with the light-hearted information coming through as well. We all need laughter; over time, the messages had a healthy balanced tone about them.

Grandmother's Symbols

Many times, when I had a reading myself from another medium, my maternal grandmother would come through. The reader would say that I received my spiritual gifts from her. This was repeated so many times that I eventually could not doubt it, but in life, I had no evidence of this. My mother's mum was a Methodist. Spirituality was not relevant to any of our lives other than we went to church. Certainly, the subject of the afterlife was something never talked about. My grandmother, mother and I were brought up to attend church. I knew her family had initially come from the Truro area of Cornwall two generations earlier in the 1850s. I had my own feeling that I had Irish stock in my family and wondered if it came through her side of the family. A few hundred years ago, the Irish used to go to Cornwall to work in the tin mines. I had no evidence of this but just went on a hunch.

In her day, my grandmother was raised to be almost a 'Victorian lady' and was sent to a ladies' college in Adelaide, South Australia, in her twenties. They would have picnics, play tennis and bridge, and it was insisted that everything was done properly. She married my grandfather, who was an Australian farmer. His people were from Devon and had been tenant farmers in the 1850s.

Their farm in Australia went under the grand name of Unley Park. Old cartwheels were nailed to either side of the entrance gates, which opened onto a long lane leading to the farmstead. The original house was a humble weatherboard cottage, which was added to over the years. It must have been a hard life for my grandmother. I know my grandfather truly loved his farm and the outdoor life.

When my mother moved back to her hometown, near the farm, for a year when my parents had separated, we were split up between relatives until my mother found a home of her own. At times, I got the distinct impression that my grandmother didn't like me, so I was puzzled as to why she would come through from the spirit side so often. Perhaps in life, she was just stressed that we had invaded her house, and she was concerned for her daughter's future. Her son had taken over the running of the farm, so my grandparents had moved into the nearby town for their retirement. After passing, my grandmother took it upon herself to become a spirit guide.

A large bookcase with a fish tank divided the lounge from the dining room. A sliding door was at one end. My grandmother would get angry with us if she caught us watching the television in the next room while looking through the fish tank whilst we were eating our dinner!

When I was in the development class, it was explained how spirit would often work with symbols. For this reason, it was suggested that we build up a 'filing cabinet' of symbols to make it easier for the spirit to work, a kind of shorthand. Most of my symbols were obvious, but there were a few that were very obtuse.

It was on one of the weekend workshops in Eastbourne. This time, I was with the medium Billy Cook. Billy explained about symbols. We were then given pen and paper. Firstly, we wrote down a series of words or phrases on the left. He then opened us up with a guided visualisation. We were then left with our guides and inspirers to show us the symbol for each word or phrase that was written down.

Some of my symbols left me scratching my head. I wrote them down the same way they had been given to me by the spirit world. I had asked spirit for a symbol of a person being hard on themselves, spirit showed me the Eiffel Tower. "How weird," I thought. From then on, whenever I saw the Eiffel Tower in my mind's eye, I knew that the recipient could sometimes be too hard on themselves, and they were their own worst critic.

Another symbol which baffled me for years was the symbol for 'growth through hardship.' For this, spirit gave me a broken fish tank! Ok, I went with it. I received other more obvious symbols:

A giraffe for having a goal for the future,

A stork for (of course) a baby on the way,

An iron for smoothing things out,

A bunch of violets for a recent passing.

Mediumship changes, and today, some of these symbols never or hardly ever come up. Spirit has also added to these symbols. Now, if spirit shows me an alligator bag, I know someone around the person in question is being snappy! Spirit often mentioned Coronation Street and the three ducks on the wall, which I now realise is a shorthand way of saying get organised or "get your ducks in a row!"

Many, many years later, after my mother had died, an aunt sent me some notes that my grandmother had handwritten about my mother when my mum was still a small child. These notes were amusing. My aunt apologised that some of the writing was blurred, explaining that the papers had been kept under the fish tank and the water had leaked on the notes.

That was spirit's message to me so many years later, that I would have growth through hardship. A broken fish tank! They had given me the symbol so many years earlier.

The meaning of the Eiffel Tower symbol became apparent, too, about 15 years after the first exercise with Billy. I was going through a box of photos that I had taken when I first arrived in the UK. I was staying with the family in Kent as a Man Friday. Their cousins had a Danish au pair, and it was suggested that we go to France together for a holiday weekend. It would also give us the opportunity to bring back as much duty-free cheese and wine as we could fit into our backpacks.

On that weekend, we went to the Eiffel Tower, and I had made a move on the nanny and got the cold shoulder. I was mortified at the time as I had embarrassed myself and gave myself a very hard time. In the box of photographs was a picture of the nanny with a view of the Eiffel Tower in the background. My subconscious had remembered it.

With the violets, which represented a recent passing, an Aunt arrived at the hospital when my mother was dying, holding a bunch of violets for my mum. My heart sank. Another sign that came to reality years and years after I had been given it in Billy's class.

Peter Gibbs

I met The medium Peter Gibbs through the London Spiritual mission church in Notting Hill Gate. It turned out he lived in Battersea. At the time, I lived near Battersea station, so I often went around for a cup of tea and a chat, or should I say, a cup of tea and to listen! Peter would put the kettle on and then talk non-stop. I could never get a word in edgeways.

Although a medium, Peter wasn't what I called a 'leaky medium', meaning he didn't give messages at random times as some mediums did. He saved it all for the platform. He was switched off until he was on the platform to work. He made up for it with his endless chatter. Peter did slip up just the once though. In the middle of pouring the tea, without pausing for breath, he told me that it was my grandmother who gave me the names. "I never get names," I thought to myself, but I thanked him anyway. A few months later, I was doing a demonstration at the SAGB. One name came through, then another, then another and another until seven names had been reeled off. It was like a roll call. The woman knew every single person: her seven brothers! After that, I would often get names. Soon after, I would get flowers, which were also names: Daisy, Violet, Iris, Daphne, Poppy, Rose and Ivy. This type of information would come in phases and, after a while, only come through occasionally.

Sometimes, when a spate of very common names were given off, like George, Mary, William, Stan, spirit would give a more uncommon name to give the reading more credibility, for example, Percy or Bartholomew!

From all my classes, I knew a few full-time mediums. Most of them were fine mediums and in exactly the right job. The medium, Billy Cook, who had done the session on the symbols, had lived a colourful life in the Navy. He would brag that he had lived a life of sex, drugs and rock and roll. As he would say himself, "I bring through all the alcoholics, prostitutes and gamblers. Like attracts like." Billy was so outrageous that a lot of churches refused to book him. But I could see his point. He could help living people with drink and drug problems as it was in his sphere. He had lived it, so could relate to others with a similar background. He would always get everyone laughing with his bawdy humour!

There was a time when I thought to myself that I hadn't had any guidance for a while. Almost immediately, I awoke from a dream with the message, "You have not been cleaning your teeth!" I wondered why spirit would tell me such a trivial thing when I could be given something so much more profound. Years later, my teeth are in bad condition, and I sorely regret not paying more attention to them. So, the 'trivial' dream had not been trivial one bit. Spirit people can be very 'down to earth' and practical.

Proof They Are with You

A spirit will often tell you of things that you have just been doing or what you have been thinking about to prove that they had been with you. One lady spirit showed me a teapot in the shape of a house, a silver sugar dish with a hanging spoon and a purple bowl within it. "I have the teapot that shape and the silver sugar bowl, the lady I was reading for said. She told me later that these were things in her loft that she had meant to bring down as they had sentimental memories.

The years rolled by. About every second Sunday was spent serving a church. I had started by calling a few churches and quickly got a handful of bookings. Then other churches would hear about you as a 'new medium,' and a circuit of churches soon built up. A church would usually only book you twice a year, so the congregation saw different people. One church that booked me a lot was the Wimbledon Spiritualist Church.

So many times, I found myself thinking that all this was such a strange thing that I had found myself doing. Once or twice, I mentioned it to people in my 'normal' world, and I would always get an odd reaction, so I just kept it to myself. I never told my family. I was leading a kind of double life.

I had become one of those people who spoke in a 'strange language' that I had mocked all those years ago. I was careful to keep my feet in both camps and continued with my other life. This dual existence eventually became the new normal for me.

After a good Sunday service, it would set me up for the week. I would walk and drive around with the feel-good factor all week. I felt that I had helped somebody, and when the spirit ran through me, it left me feeling content. As my connections with the spirits slowly became stronger, the more relaxed I was, the more natural it all seemed, and I settled into my own style of working.

When I started to work at the churches, at first, it didn't seem easy to carry the connection of spirit for such a long time, to work continuously from one person to the next for what was usually an hour and up to an hour and a half. The church services were easier as the clairvoyance was about forty minutes, and the rest was spent with prayers, hymns, readings and an address. The church service also set the tone for the clairvoyance. With time, my strength grew and grew, my spiritual muscles gradually strengthened, and some evenings I didn't want to stop! I did have a habit of staying a long while with one person, and some churches preferred me to do readings for several people.

When I started working with the churches, someone remarked, "It is when you are working as a medium that you really learn the language of spirit." It had just taken me 15 years of complete dedication to get to that point!

After a while, I noticed that I would often see the very object that I had given to somebody as a fact the next day or a day or two later. Once, I mentioned a honeypot in the shape of a beehive. I saw this the next day in the window of a charity shop. Another time, I saw a traditional gypsy caravan, and again, I saw one the very next day. A Saint Bernard dog, a man with one leg, you couldn't make it up!

I told a friend about it, and he said it was just a coincidence, like when you hear a new word you have not heard before and then see it everywhere as it is now in your consciousness. I could see his point, but when it was experiences that were very obtuse, I couldn't put it down to coincidences.

Another time, I had told a lady that she hated roundabouts. She confirmed, "Yes, that's why I don't drive." About ten days later, I was coming out of my office and walking towards my van. There was a man standing beside the van, and I knew he wanted to talk to me. I had worked a very long day and didn't want to talk to anyone.

"Are you the gardener?" he asked.

"Yes," I replied, becoming instantly wary.

"Well, it's about the roundabout at the end of the main road," he went on to explain. Would you be interested in planting it up?" He asked, saying that in return, I would be able to put up an advertising sign. I immediately remembered the reading about hating roundabouts. I made up my mind in an instant, and hastily told him that I wasn't interested!

Morse Code

It was usual for the medium to sit in a quiet room before the service to link into the spirit world and to meditate. There, I waited until the chairperson offered me a cup of tea, which I gratefully accepted. I would joke to other mediums that we were paid with a cup of tea and a biscuit for our work. This was very much the currency of our business and sometimes a box of tissues!

One afternoon, I had a booking at a church in Windsor. I left in plenty of time but hit standstill traffic as the Westway, one of London's main arterial roads, was shut for major road works. I tried another route and realised I would be horribly late as all the routes out were gridlocked. Sunday afternoon traffic in London can be much worse than in the week, even without the road closures.

I was stuck in traffic and thought, "Gosh, I'm not going to make it." Suddenly, just as I had that thought, there was a sharp stab of pain in my heart. I let out a cry. I realised that I had a man with me who had died of a heart attack, and he was waiting to come through with a message for his wife. I realised I would make it to the church and should not give up. The man did come through and gave a message to his wife. I told him off for giving me his pain so strongly.

Since then, those kinds of experiences have been tempered right down, but this is one of the pitfalls of being empathic. The congregation had patiently waited for an hour and a half.

Qualities of Mediumship

After years of working, I noticed that sometimes a sitter would have to come a few times before a really strong and profound link came through for them. I wondered why the person didn't come through in the first sitting. I think the sitter had to be prepared for what was said, and the 'run-up' readings, so to speak, allowed that. The same could be said, spirit side, and perhaps the spiritual energy had to build up for them as well.

There was a lady at a fair who came to the public demonstration. She had people who lived in Naples, within sight of Vesuvius, the volcano of Pompeii infamy. It turned out that a 'volcano had erupted' in her very own family. Later the same day, she came with her daughter, and they both had one-to-ones with me, which were full of information.

The other medium who was supposed to be working with me that day couldn't make it, so I did two slots of public work. This same woman who had already received two readings was in the audience, and spirit went straight to her.

I thought this odd at first, after all the information that had already been given. Still, a spirit came through, and a lady spirit-side apologised to her. The woman in the audience burst into tears. It turned out the lady in the spirit world had fallen out with her over an inheritance and had become very nasty. She came through with a very specific message. A great healing took place, and I felt that both the spirit lady and the lady on earth could move on.

There was a Portuguese lady who had come for several sittings at Clapham before her disabled nephew came through and said, "Let me go." Why didn't he come through in the first reading? I think all parties needed to be ready to move on. Who said that the fruit doesn't fall until it is ripe?

When I had only recently started out doing the readings, I had an evening of clairvoyance in a hall in Kent, and the following day, I would do one to ones. I had three ladies booked in; a mother and her two daughters. Now, I didn't know that until afterwards, that they were all related. They all came for readings for the same thing: to link with their father and husband. Again, I didn't know this until afterwards. The mother came in first. Try as I might, I could hardly get a thing for her. I did say that she had ringed a calendar date, but that was pretty much all she could accept in the reading.

The first daughter came in, and I got a variety of information, but only a little to do with her father. Then, the second daughter came in. Her father came through loud and clear, and evidence after evidence flowed through, even advice about her next job. I questioned why he had come through so unequally to his relatives.

With that third reading, the lady's energy allowed the connection. With the man's wife, as much as they may have had a happy marriage, there was just not an energetic connection. So, from the spirit side of life, it was impossible for him to come through. This was a great learning curve for me that you bring with you your own reading.

A Run of Elephants!

At another early demonstration, this time in Milton Keynes, I was working with a woman when all of a sudden, I had an elephant spirit beside me. Wow, when you feel the energy of an animal as graceful, loyal, and intelligent as an elephant, I can tell you it is an absolutely wonderful experience.

"Can you take an elephant in the spirit world?" I said in disbelief to the woman.

"Oh yes," she said, almost casually. It turned out she had worked with a circus elephant. Spirit then showed me an elephant figurine that she had in her home, which she confirmed as a seat in that shape.

Sometime later, I was at the SAGB. "I'm with the person who has ridden an elephant, " I said incredulously. A person then accepted, but spirit pulled me around to face the piano player, Latchme.

"I have ridden an elephant," she said. "My Grandfather owned them!"

In the same vein, I went on a holiday to Morocco. On the plane on the way back, I felt an elephant with me. "How strange," I thought; I don't know where I picked him up. Again, it was a lovely energy and one that I was so happy to have around me, a blessing. I didn't understand why he was around me, though, if, in fact, there needed to be a reason. A few days later, I had an intense dream about an Indian elephant. I have a feeling that I have dealt with elephants in my past life. Why else would they come around me? Elephants never forget.

Barcelona

Almost as soon as I became a working medium, Peter Gibbs gave me a call asking if I would like to do a demonstration in Barcelona. Of course, I said yes. We flew off, and I was billeted by a Spanish couple. Again, I was nervous, but I was gaining confidence. His friends had booked out a hall, and it was packed to capacity for this ticket-only event. Peter started the evening, and then my time came to link in. There was a translator, so there was a pause between each piece of information as it was translated into Spanish. This time-lapse was helpful as it gave me time to get the next piece of information. I linked immediately to a young chap whose parents were in the audience. He came through with various pieces of information. He started to say how his parents did not get on with their neighbours.

"Oh yes," they agreed. Then, the boy showed me barbed wire.

"You don't get on with them so badly that you should put barbed wire around the house?"

"Oh yes," she said. We already have!" The audience erupted in laughter as they saw the funny side of it.

The Spanish treated us marvellously, and it was a wonderful experience. I was introduced to the audience as a beginner. "You're not a beginner now," they said after that message.

Back in London, it was back to gardening by day and demonstrations at night, my unusual double life.

Hope

Again, I was thinking of giving up the mediumship. I was still finding it hard to integrate it into normal life or to bring both aspects of my dual existence closer together. When I finally had the courage to tell people what I did, I would often get a strange reaction. People either think you are odd, that you can read their thoughts or that you are constantly 'picking things up', exactly what I had thought when I met my first medium. This is not the case at all. Anyway, I was having these thoughts as I was driving along at work and "I love you so much, Peter" ran through my head out of nowhere. As I said, it was not usual for me to get a communication whilst I was operating in my normal mode. Peter was a young Hungarian guy who was working for me as a gardener. "Wow," I thought, "he must have someone in spirit looking out for him, or he has powerful spirit guides!" I was almost jealous, hearing it so strongly. Why didn't they ever tell me that!

Later that day, the phone beeped with a text message. It was Peter. He texted that his father had died that day, and he had to go back to Hungary. I told him to take as long as he needed and that his father loved him very much. His father had reached out to me as he knew I may hear his final words. I decided to keep going with the mediumship after this experience.

Chapter Seven

EXTRA ORDINARY

Israel & Anya

I had wanted to visit Israel for many years. I knew that the yoga group had gone quite a few years earlier, so I thought they could recommend a few 'must-see' places I could visit. I mentioned that I was intending to go. "Oh, it is such a bad time to go," I was told. I asked a few other people and was put off every time it was mentioned. With the discouragement, I postponed the trip.

A few years later, the desire arose again to make the trip. A relationship had just ended badly, leaving me heartbroken and empty, and I just wanted to get away. I again asked members of the same yoga group and received the same response: "You won't meet Anya."

It turned out that a previous yoga member who lived in Israel was travelling to London at the very time I was due to leave. I had never met her as I didn't know about the group when she was a member. I asked another member, again expecting them to tell me which places to visit. Still, I was met with the same response: lousy timing with the instability in the region as America was just preparing to invade Iraq, and not meeting Anya of course.

I was far more determined this time, and I wasn't about to be put off again. I viewed the trip as way more important than meeting someone I had never met before. I decided to go. A gardening client had a property in Tel Aviv and recommended I give her address if I had any issues getting into the country. Sure enough, I was grilled by border control. They seemed to think it was peculiar that a tourist would want to visit Israel at that time. Eventually, I was allowed through, and once through border control, I stepped into a different world altogether.

Now, being a romantic and having a childhood of going to Sunday school, I had a notion that Israel may still hold the flavour of a desert oasis, with people riding donkeys and palm trees waving in the air, colourful people living in mud houses. The reality that greeted me, the concrete jungle of a thoroughly modern Israel, could not have been starker.

I didn't arrive with any set travel plans, and after a short time in Tel Aviv, I left for Haifa. Here, I saw the world's largest Bahia temple. In Haifa, a bus bomb had gone off two weeks earlier, and the tense atmosphere was palpable. I was struck by the Jewish /Arab divide.

At the youth hostel where I was staying, I met another lone traveller, and we decided to travel together for a while. We set off for Kirat-Shamona, on the border with Lebanon. Here, we were stopped by a jeep full of soldiers asking us to produce our passports as we were far too near to the border. We were near the beautiful Golan Heights. I parted from my companion, who wanted to go to Syria, and I set off to Galilee. It was very pretty there, but I couldn't feel a 'Jesus' presence, which I had hoped for. I soon grew bored, not knowing the language and having nothing to read, I decided to return to Tel Aviv, where I bought some English books, before setting off to Jerusalem.

I fell in love with Old Jerusalem and stayed in a youth hostel in an ancient old stone house. As it was wintertime, it was like staying in an ice box. These houses were not built for cold weather. I hadn't done my research and was ignorant that it could get bitterly cold in parts of Israel in the winter. I set off to many great sites, such as the Golden Gate, the Garden of

Gethsemane, and the Arab Market. This was more like it and akin to the atmosphere I had been expecting. Having "done" Jerusalem and, more to the point, getting chilled to the bone, I decided to head for Eilat, which I was told was a lot warmer.

Another bus trip later, I was well on my way, travelling through the desert. Again, I had not done my homework, having been happy to travel to Israel and 'follow my nose', so although it was obvious to others that we were approaching the Dead Sea, it was not until we were driving alongside it that it dawned on me where we were. I realised that I must quickly decide whether to get off or not. That didn't take long: I would probably never be passing that way again. I would get off.

The bus passed by a small national park alongside a youth hostel, next to a kibbutz, with the sea on the other side, then a car park and a few shops where all the tourists stopped to gaze out over the ocean to the orange range of mountains in Jordan on the far side.

The bus drove on for what seemed an age before stopping near the private health resorts which the Dead Sea is so famous for. With my rucksack, I headed back towards the youth hostel. When asking for a bed, I was also invited to pay an extra 70 Shekels for a Shabbat meal. Having no food on me, I hastily agreed.

It was a modern hostel set beside a national park that held the legend of the location where David had fought Goliath. With mealtime approaching, I went into the dining hall and was sat on an English-speaking table. There, I chatted away with two Jewish-English girls who had both married Israeli-Jewish men. There was also a Jewish-English girl who had a Bedouin boyfriend. She was off to visit him on the Sinai Peninsula, just over the border and invited me along. I immediately scrapped my plans to go to Eilat and agreed to go to the resort in Sinai instead. I had my books to read, and I had I wanted to get away from it all.

I was aware that by going to Egypt, it meant that not one person in the world who knew me knew where I was. I was completely off the grid. As I was wanting to get over a heartbreak, this seemed like an ideal opportunity to heal.

The evening meal was delicious, and the conversation flowed easily. One of the English-Jewish girls invited me for a walk along the 'beach' as she called it, after the meal. We met up outside the hostel and headed off towards the shores of the Dead Sea. As we strolled along, I noticed how the orange of the mountains looming up on the other side of the lake were the same orange as those at Flaming Mountain in China. The second thing I noticed was the particular kind of stuffy heat. I guessed this was because we were at the lowest point on earth below sea level. This also reminded me of the heat at Flaming Mountain, the second lowest point below sea level.

"You Know," I remarked," this place reminds me of the Taklamakan Desert and Flaming Mountain in China".

She looked at me. "Do you know a woman called Judith?" She asked.

"Is your name Anya?" I replied.

Her mouth dropped. "How do you know my name?"

"I was told about you before I left!" I responded in a 'smart alec' but truthful way.

It turned out that due to the impending Iraq war, Anya had cancelled her holiday to London and had gone to the Dead Sea for a break instead. It was funny that as soon as I mentioned that remote place, she mentioned the person who had taken me there. I knew straight away that it was Anya. There were 11 million people living in Israel, so what were the chances of us meeting, especially as all I had was her first name? She had never heard of me. I was so glad I had the courage of my convictions and went ahead with the trip.

I parted the next day and took the bus with my new companion. We set off for Taba, in Egypt. Once through the border, it wasn't long before we were driving past many deserted beach hut resorts. A few years earlier, they had been full of Israelis, but because of fresh instability in the region, they were now all empty. We got off the bus at one of these resorts, which looked like all the rest, and now a ghost town.

Apart from the guy's girlfriend, I was the only guest! I had little to do apart from reading a book I had bought in Tel Aviv. I can't explain it, but being alone and completely anonymous helped me tremendously to heal and put myself back together. One day, getting bored of lounging around the camp, I made it my day's plan to climb one of the many mountains behind me. There was a thin band, almost a sand strip, with a road and nothing more before a range of cone-like mountains that studded the coastline and stretched out for as far as the eye could see. I picked one and set off after lunch, taking my book with me. I didn't see anybody as I made my way over to the slope and started to climb. There were no animals or humans, and I had a day of complete solitude. Up and up, I went, eventually reaching the summit. As I reached the pinnacle, two butterflies fluttered past. These were the only living creatures I had seen since I left the camp.

The mountain was like a cone, with the top only about six feet across before dropping down the other side. There were similar peaks that stretched off for miles and miles into the distance as I looked over the peninsular. It was completely barren. There was a stone cairn at the pinnacle, so I found a flat stone and added another rock. With nothing left to do, I sat down and continued reading my novel, sat atop the mountain! After an hour or two, it dawned on me that I had better start down the mountain, or else I would not reach the camp before dark. Halfway down, I picked up speed as I realised I wouldn't beat the sunset. The sun went down quickly, and it wasn't long before I was clambering over the rocks in the dark. I am one of those people who is comfortable walking in the dark. I can't say I can see in the dark exactly, but I managed to scramble down the rocky terrain quite easily. A straight-down direction was all that was required, so it wasn't as though I would get lost. I would reach the sea and find the camp.

As I hit the sea, I was one camp away from the one where I was staying. There was a group of Bedouins sitting around a campfire on the beach. I went down to the sea to wash off some of the day's sweat and made my way over to the men. It turned out that when they saw me in the distance, washing in the sea, they thought I was a rebel gunrunner who had come in from the mountains. I thought it very funny that I was assumed to be a terrorist, as I wouldn't hurt a fly! I made my way over to my hut. A day later, I set off back to Israel and to the airport home.

My yoga friends didn't ask about the trip, but I did tell them that I had met Anya. The trip had helped me heal and move on with my life. It had been the one time I had really wanted to be alone and be 'off the grid', so to speak, even if only for a short time. I felt it was a way of putting myself back together, and the solitude had worked!

Some months later, I went to see the famous medium Gordon Smith at The London Spiritual Mission. It was an evening of clairvoyance, and the church was packed to capacity as it always was when he was there. I was sat at the back. Gordon came to me and started to talk about the Orange Mountains (Sinai) and doing a ritual (putting the stone on the cairn). "Your grandmother was with you then," he said. I thought immediately of the butterflies. "Damn," I thought, "I wanted to be alone!"

This proved to me that we are never, ever alone!

Who is Dorothy?

The chairwoman warned me that two regulars in the congregation had a reputation for being difficult and were both very deaf. I got up on the platform, and there in the front row were the two old ladies glaring at me.

At Stansted, a tutor had told us never to let anyone in the congregation take the energy away from you; so conscious of this, every time the women muttered something to each other or rustled their plastic bags, I would stop what I was doing, turn to them smiling and say "Are you OK?" or

"Are you alright ladies," or words to that effect. Well, these two were a nightmare; they rustled and rustled, and being deaf, they continuously shouted comments to each other. It was straight out of a comedy sketch when they proceeded to get boiled sweets out from their bags, noisily unwrapping them, of course, before loud sucking sounds ensued. At one point, one turned to the other and said, "HE'S DREADFUL!"

I couldn't believe her gall. Once again, I turned to them and asked, "All right, ladies?" Lo and behold, as I said this to them, a spirit drew close for one of them and told me that they had also been deaf.

"I don't mean to be rude," I shouted, "but there is someone in the spirit world who was also deaf."

"Yes," one said, "my mother." Lots of evidence followed.

"You have just changed the water in a vase of flowers as it was getting really smelly," I said.

"I did that today," she replied.

"Spirit are telling me that your emotions are like the water, and you need to let go of a situation as the emotions have gone stale. You must put new emotions in yourself," I told her.

"Yes, yes," she said, "I can take that. I've been told before that I need to let go."

I had no idea myself of what the lady's situation was as spirit weren't telling me: none of my business or anyone else's there. Other information came through, all of which she accepted. Spirit had drawn close and suddenly said, "Dorothy."

"Who's Dorothy?" I asked. The other lady nearly jumped out of her chair. She pointed to herself nervously. The expression on her face was priceless. I thought that she was going to run out of the building!

I hope the lady let go of her situation. I could see that in its extreme, holding onto a negative emotion can, and does, cause disease. Unease can potentially create illness. When you are in the middle of a situation that is dear to your heart, and it has gone sour, it can be very hard to realise when the right point has come to give it up. It can then become stagnant and go septic. Sometimes, it takes great courage to shake off what has become shackles. You know you have done it when you get that sense of freedom back and that lightness returns to your step. As we are all creatures of habit, it is very easy, especially as we get older, to hold on to the negative as well as the positive. A refresh is never a bad thing!

It sounds corny, but "when life gives you lemons, make lemonade!"

Violet, Ivy and Daphne

A message finished, and I asked spirit for the next 'link'. Quickly, they fired Violet, Ivy, and Daphne. I didn't know who I was going to.

"Who can take those three names?" I asked. Two people put their hands up. I went back to spirit for some more information.

"They know people who have been in trouble with the law," I called out. Both accepted it. Then I had a knowing of who I was with, so I thanked the lady and went to the gentleman. The evidence and message then followed.

A few days later, I was working in Whitstable. Halfway through a message, spirit said the three names again. I dutifully repeated them: Violet, Ivy and Daphne. Sure enough, they were accepted. The following day, I did Saturday night at Margate at St Peter's Memorial Hall. I think you know what I got, well not quite... Ivy and Daphne. "Stop right there," I said to the audience, then told them that I had got these names twice before and spirit hadn't told me the third name, but I now know that you can, in fact, take the third name, "Violet", I cried out. "Yes, I can take a Violet in spirit," a lady said.

I think spirit were teaching me a very important lesson; that I can't always expect to be spoon-fed the information, and if they can give it to me in a shorthand fashion, then they will. As if to back this up, at the service where I first got these three names, I was well into the session when talking to a woman.

I simply said, "Spirit are telling me that you have been able to take a lot of the information for yourself from the last few messages for others."

"Yes," she said.

"Spirit are telling me that it is for you to accept," I went on. "The messages are for you as well." As if to confirm it, spirit then gave her some evidence just for her.

Strangely, I have done a couple of services where someone has come up to me afterwards and said that they could understand every single piece of information from start to finish that I had given to four or five people over the course of an hour and a half!

One to Ones

After I felt I had cut my teeth with services and evenings of clairvoyance, I started doing one-to-one readings. Thinking the one-to-one readings were at the same time as services, I turned up over half an hour late for my first session. Not a good start! I didn't feel particularly tuned into spirit. Debbie gave me a cup of tea and plenty of time to 'open up'.

When my first person came in, plenty of information flowed, and I was happy with the specific evidence. The same was true for the second person. The third person was a 50-something lady from Portugal who spoke no English, so her 14-year-old niece had come along as a translator. Various information came through. I saw a safe being opened and papers taken out.

I said to the woman, "Important papers need to be signed."

"Yes," she said to her niece.

I got the name Robert, and she explained that she had to sign a restaurant over, and the name of the restauranteur was Robert. Her mother was in spirit, and my heart went out to this lady, as she missed her mum so much. Tears rolled down her cheeks as I said that her mother touched her hair and that she really loved to have her hair done.

I felt for this Portuguese woman; she really thought I would bring through spirit, and I sensed her need, the empty chasm in her life. I have to say that I felt a pressure to fill that gap and bring spirit through. I should not have worried, spirit came up with the goods. She had a husband she had adored who had died some years earlier.

"Let me go," he said". I understand," she answered. This was the third time a spirit person had said, "Let me go." In the spirit world, souls also progress.

From what I have been told by spirit, a person's thoughts can hold a soul back. Another was for a disabled child, this disabled child's soul was not disabled, but if relatives kept thinking of it as such, it could tie the soul to the condition in their earthly existence. When you go to spirit, this is simply not relevant any more. In Australian aboriginal culture, once a person dies, their name is not mentioned again as they believe it holds their soul close to the earth.

I was surprised that the next sitter was the 14-year-old translator girl. I thought that she was too young for a reading, but spirit came through brilliantly. Wow! Spirit laughed 'their heads off' as they told me she had recently been caught eating sweets in class at school. Spirit said, "Well, what do you expect when the class is so quiet and you then proceed to unwrap the sweet from the crinkly wrapper!" We both fell about laughing at that one. It is amazing when you link with spirit and expect to hear something so profound and God-like, and what do you get: being caught out eating sweets! Other good evidence ensued, like a crystal bowl with a silver-trimmed lid. This had belonged to her grandparents and was their way of saying they were the main communicators. It was their "calling card".

After the fourth reading, I made the mistake of thinking how well it was all going. Well, then, it was a struggle. The last one was a breeze, however. It was with a spiritual lady, so the information just flowed and flowed.

One guy I spoke to, George, an elderly chap, I just got that "You have had the most amazing experience to do with spirit that confirmed without a doubt the existence of a spirit world and a higher power, an angelic experience."

"Yes." Was his response. I have never seen or felt an angel myself, but they were sometimes mentioned in readings and were always accepted. In the last reading I did, the woman said I had gone back 250 years in her family history!

While doing a demonstration at the SAGB, I felt drawn to a woman. I started by saying she had known a trapeze artist. She agreed with this. I then said there was a guy who worked with a submarine. She accepted this. I then went to her friend, who was sitting next to her, and gave her three names.

"Now you are scaring me," she said, "They are three brothers!" Well, that put me off. I was amazed myself, and I didn't know they were brothers. The demonstration went on. It was one of those where spirit flowed abundantly. In one of my last connections, I asked a woman, "Do you have a memory of someone stepping backwards and falling down a hatch?"

"No," she said. I let it go. After the service, the woman I went to initially came up to me and said that she could accept everything I had said for the whole service. She said that her husband worked on a submarine and had phoned her the evening before and told her that a man had died that night on the submarine as he had stepped backwards and fell down a hatch. The lady told me he left a wife and a small baby behind. I felt terrible as I hadn't got that across.

Another time at a demonstration in Kent, I said, "I'm with the person who recently put chrysanthemums on a grave." A woman answered immediately, and spirit rushed through. I felt like bursting into tears; the passing was tragic and very, very recent. "It's very raw," I said. "She wants to say, 'You're my star.'" "We just brought her a star for the grave," the mother said. A year later, I was in the same part of Kent, and this woman came up to me and said that it was the first anniversary of her daughter's death, and she hoped her daughter would come through. I can never repeat a connection 'on request' as the spirit people decide who will come through, not the messenger. Alas, I did not connect with her daughter a second time.

Arthur Findlay College

I went to a week's course of mediumship training. This is the "Hogwarts" College of Mediumship. The week-long course was very intensive; after living in a spiritual "bubble", it was quite challenging to return to life as usual the week after. At the end of the week, we had to demonstrate individually and get a critique from the teaching medium. I started off with an elephant's foot as an ashtray. To the medium's amazement, this was accepted. Spirit could give me this information because, as a boy, I knew a woman who had spent most of her life in Zimbabwe and had an elephant's foot in her home! As this was stored in my memory banks, the spirit people could bring it forward into my consciousness and use it as a message.

The Pillar of Light

Almost all mediums recount stories of seeing spirit as a child or having imaginary friends who turned out to be spirit people. I never did or at least that is what I thought initially. My best friend at school often told spooky ghost stories, but I wasn't particularly interested in them. Looking back, however, I think I had invisible aboriginal spirit friends who influenced me. When I was around 10, I would daydream about living self-sufficiently in the bush. Older, I would imagine cutting my chest and putting ash into the wound. I didn't know at the time, but the Tasmanian aborigine would do this as well as their mainland counterparts as a rite of passage when coming of age. Why would I imagine such a thing? I revised my thinking. My home town was built around a sacred site, "The Bluff", which was a promontory of rock. I had spent my first seven years where the aborigines had been re-homed on Flanders Island.

My school friend and I got our driving licences at 16, and with our newfound freedom, we would go to early colonial homes. We were both obsessed with antiques and loved the old houses, which Chris had an excellent knowledge of. If they were abandoned on a farm, it was all the more interesting to go and explore for ourselves.

There was one near Elizabethtown, which was built in 1834 across the highway from my father's farm. It was called Whiteford Hills and was surrounded by fine 150-year-old European trees. It was dilapidated, and the farmer had no interest in restoration. There was another near Bothwell called Sherwood, which was built in the Georgian style, a fashion that remained in Tasmania long after tastes had changed in Britain. This house was often used for film sets. Many of these houses were still private homes, while a few were owned by the National Trust. These would have been more like large farmhouses or rectories in the UK. In Tasmania, they were its country houses.

There was one at Mole Creek set well away from the road from where one could just see its roof in the distance. Stood between this house and the road was the much newer farmhouse with a dirt track leading from the main road. We chose to ignore the sign on the gate that read: "PRIVATE, KEEP OUT" and agreed to set off at five in the morning to arrive on the outlying road at six when the countryside was still sleeping. We parked away from the farmhouse and walked a quarter circle, steering clear of the inhabited house so that we could have a look at the abandoned mansion. There was a morning mist as we made our way over the dewy paddocks, navigating a few barbed wire fences.

Before too long, we came up to the house and were surprised to find it in such remarkably good order. It was brick built, with a large veranda flanking three sides, and cried out High Victorian. We stood on what was once the front lawn, gazing at the facade. Suddenly, a pillar of light, the height of a person, grew up in front of us between the house and ourselves. I grabbed Chris's arm and pointed in disbelief, "LOOK," before turning on my heels and fleeing! We sprinted past the farmstead, dogs coming out and barking a warning at us, running on as fast as we could, over the farmgate and back to the car. Getting into the car, I asked Chris between great gasping breaths of air, "Did you see that?" before gunning the engine and speeding off down the highway, away from the house and whatever it was we had seen. He didn't answer.

Perhaps it was a ghost. Looking back, I think it was a spirit guide. We were not supposed to be on the land, and I think we were getting a ticking off, using our fear to move us along. It certainly worked! That was my first paranormal experience.

Psychic Fayre in Australia

Once, when visiting my mother in Tasmania, I saw that a psychic fair was taking place in my hometown at the RSL (Retired Serviceman's League), so I called the organiser and asked if I could do readings.

He booked me for half a day. I told my mother that I was going to a crystal fair. This wasn't entirely untrue, as there were stalls selling an impressive range of crystals. I was billed as a visiting medium from London, which all sounded very grand, and I was soon fully booked up.

I had mixed success. With one lady, I could not get a thing, so I sent her back to the front desk to see someone else. One lady's mother communicated beautifully and clearly. A cat came through for another lady, who was amazed that a pet could come through, though I now take this for granted myself.

A lady whose mother had passed sat down in front of me. I took my energy up to spirit. All I saw was smoke.

"Smoke," I said, relaying what I was seeing. I repeated this two more times, "Smoke, smoke," as this was all I was seeing.

She looked at me blankly.

"Come on, spirit," I said, "give me something else." I went into it again, and this time, it was a smoke-filled room. I relayed to the lady how everyone in the family used to smoke. You would have social evenings where, by the time the evening was finished, the room was filled with smoke. She agreed to this. Then her mother spoke of an extension, which her daughter was having added to her house, a cruise... the information went on, and the lady left very satisfied. A couple of days later, the whole state was covered in smoke from over 100 bushfires throughout the island. The smoke got so bad it even covered tracts of the Victorian mainland. I remembered my reading and knew it was her mother hinting at what was to come.

HMS Victory & Nelson

Years earlier, I had taken a service at the Camden Town Spiritualist Church. After it finished, I felt a strong impulse to drive home through central London instead of taking my usual route home. I drove off and found myself driving around Trafalgar Square. The unadorned plinth had a work of art on it; it was a model of HMS Victory in a glass bottle. I knew I was guided to see it.

A few weeks before that, I was at the Eastbourne weekend workshop. This weekend, the teacher, Mary Armour, decided to do something different: trance. My turn came. I did my best to let go and allow someone to come through. Other class members watched. One word came out, 'victory', and afterwards, a chap watching said he saw a galleon at the same time. Mary said I had an admiral with me!

A fortnight before that, I was driving home and saw a spirit person standing at the side of the road. It was an 18th-century gentleman wearing a big coat and a three-sided hat that sailors wore! When I got home, I told my flatmate what I had seen. He was not impressed, telling me to keep that to myself or people would think I was mad! It wasn't as though this kind of thing happened often. I was in 'normal' mode and certainly hadn't been thinking about anything spiritual when it happened.

After a demonstration at Sutton, where HMS Victory came up in a reading, I resolved to finally visit her. I had a clear weekend ahead of me, so I made the plan. As I walked through Waterloo station, I heard on the Tannoy "Portsmouth Harbour": a cue. Later that day, while working on a roof garden for a client, I checked my emails on my phone. There was a reply to a local choir I had applied to join. Come along, it said, we are rehearsing Hayden's 'Nelson's Mass.' Another sign, I thought!

That night, I ventured off to the pub opposite my house. The pub was packed, so I sat at a table with a reserved sign, knowing I would move on when that party arrived. I was soon moved on to a large and empty table.

After just a few minutes, a lady came and asked if she could share the table. In her next breath, I learnt that one guest soon to arrive was in the Australian Navy, whilst the other two were Australian solicitors, so I dropped the fact that I was Australian into the conversation. Her guests soon arrived, and the naval chap almost immediately told his friends he would arrange a meal on HMS Victory. One more sign. One can read signs into everything, but when you are bombarded with the same thing, it is spirit's way of making a point.

The next day, I set off by train.

I thought I might have a spiritual experience on my visit to the famous ship, but that wasn't to be the case. When I returned home, there was an envelope on the floor that had obviously been posted by hand. It was a thank you note from my office person for her Christmas present. On the front of the card was an anchor!

Sometime later, when giving a reading, I saw Nelson, and he said, "I lost an arm, but the person lost a digit." "Part of a digit," the sitter replied. In another demonstration, I saw Nelson's hat. I repeated this to the congregation. A man piped up, "My name is Nelson!" Certainly, Admiral Nelson is very active in the spirit world.

Guide in Melbourne

As my confidence grew, I thought working again in my homeland would be nice. I looked up some churches in Melbourne on the internet and wrote that I was visiting, asking if they would want me to serve their church. I had a positive response from one and had a Sunday service booked. The plane arrived on a Friday, and I booked the next flight to Tasmania for the Monday.

Sunday soon approached. I put on my uniform, a suit, and headed off to the church. My nerves really kicked in. They took services very differently in Australia and didn't use one medium but three! The first was to give the address while the others split the clairvoyance between them.

As I arrived, I met the other medium, a lady originally from Wales who would be doing the clairvoyance with me. She suggested that I go first. The church was packed to capacity. I stood up to work, shaking like a leaf! In a flash, I saw a huge man stand in the doorway; he was a Native American. His height and breadth filled the doorway. In the next instant, he was gone. Knowing that this was a spirit guide, he gave me the reassurance that (of course) all would be well.

I made my link and got a woman's husband through. Various things came through which she could accept. I then gave a short message to another, and before I knew it, my time was up. The Welsh lady got up and delivered about ten messages. Oh well, I did my best and had made my Australian debut! I was quietly proud of that.

Soon after returning to the UK, I had a spiritual residential weekend to go to, which was arranged by the Wimbledon Spiritualist Church. This was broken up into many short workshops and lectures. I went to one, and the lady came straight to me and described to a tee the Native American guide that I had seen in the church in Melbourne. This was great proof, having the man described who I had just seen standing in the doorway.

My Grandfather Materialised

After my paternal grandfather died, I half expected to see him or to hear from him in a reading. After six months, I thought it was odd that he hadn't come through. With all the classes I attended and getting so many messages, I had that expectancy.

We were in Italy near Sarzana doing the beginnings of a garden landscape, clearing olive terraces. A few weeks earlier, I had been out to visit the client and draw up plans, and this time around, I had brought a team over. It was lunchtime, and I was sitting on the terrace when I felt somebody behind me. I looked around, and there was my grandfather looking at me about 10 meters away. He was 'see-through' but almost solid. I stood up and turned around. He started to walk towards me, and as he did so, he disappeared. I turned and sat back on the terrace. Then, the energy of my grandfather washed over my head and down through my body. He 'overlaid' me.

I had a sense that I had many of his qualities and that we were quite similar. Due to a family feud, I had not spent any time with him, and though I had met him a few times, I didn't actually know him.

I remember, as a small child, he once told me to stick my tongue out, and when I did as I was told, he thumped me under the chin. I ran away, howling. My dad had said his father was a bad man. This spirit man, my grandfather, showed me very different qualities. It was a conundrum, but I didn't worry myself thinking about it.

Parsley Aunt

On another visit to Australia, I arranged with my sister to take mum travelling. We asked mum where she wanted to go, and she said back to her home town of Horsham. On the way back, we called in on her sister. We had been camping outside Horsham in the Grampian Mountains, staying in a self-catering cabin.

I did the cooking. As I loved parsley, I bought a bunch to chop some into the stew I had made. Having a lot left over, I gave this to my aunt when we arrived to stay for a few days. I think she found it amusing to be given a large bunch of parsley rather than a bunch of flowers! When we were there, my sister and brother-in-law said how much they wanted to go to a fake castle there called Kryal Castle near Ballarat. So off we all went.

At the castle, they put on re-enactments from castle life with actors and actresses entertaining the punters. There was jousting, an apothecary and they put on a play. We filed into the theatre and settled down in the gloom for the production to begin. It was a love story, and one of the characters was a sorcerer. At one point, he cast an incantation and put a variety of things in a pot, reeling them off one by one. "Wing of bat, eye of toad," the usual stuff, then he finished off the list with a joke: "And a bunch of parsley!"

"There you go, Jeff," said my aunt. It must have got back to my father as I remember later on in my holiday when I was back in Tasmania, my father was sat on the sofa holding a bunch of parsley! I don't know what story had got back to them!

Years later, when he found out what I did through videos, I visited him, and there in a bucket of water was a large bunch of parsley. That weekend, the old TV show Dallas came strongly into my mind. I dismissed it. The next day, my father, who had suffered from a stroke and could no longer speak, had written "Dallas" on a piece of paper. I realised he was communicating through thought. Had I taught him something?

Kangaroos Line the Road

On one trip back to Australia, the plane was continually delayed. It took me 72 hours to get to Launceston when it should have been around 24 hours. At first, the plane was delayed taking off, and then it was delayed in Dubai. Then, instead of flying to Melbourne, it landed in Sydney, where we changed planes, the flight changing from international to national. The plane then flew past Launceston and dropped down in the Tasmanian capital, Hobart, where it seemed to wait for an age before leaving to finally arrive in Launceston at 2 in the morning. My father and one of my sisters were waiting for me, half asleep in the car. I had phoned ahead to say I would be late, but this was still much later than that.

We drove back to my father's house, passing through tracts of bush and farmland that were lit by a full moon. I don't know when it started, but we noticed a wallaby on the side of the road, then another and then another, all on the left and all facing the road. We marvelled as we drove on, as it went on for miles and miles. "Even the queen wouldn't get such a guard of honour!" My father remarked, and he talked about it for days on end until eventually, a brother said that people would think he was mad if he kept mentioning it. It was a phenomenon. I knew it was the Tasmanian aborigines welcoming me home. I felt very lucky and blessed from that experience. I felt truly welcomed. Apart from my mother and a sister, I hadn't felt welcome many times when returning for a visit, but at least the country embraced me!

A Helping Hand

I was recommended to a large garden in Hampstead. Mrs Durga loved her garden and had a great love of flowers. We got on very well, and although we were from different cultures, I thought we somehow clicked. One day, I woke up after having a dream about her. I rang her the next morning.

"Mrs Durga, I hope you don't mind me speaking to you in this way, but last night, I had a dream about you that the energy was blocked at the base of your spine."

"Mr Hewitt," she replied, "when I was a child, I fell down the stairs and landed on my coccyx. Today, I am going to Harley Street for treatment for my back pain."

We had a great deal of respect for each other. She wasn't a well lady and had to go to Spain for treatment. Her son had announced his engagement, and Mrs Durga said there would be a party in the garden to celebrate. She left it to me to get the garden ready. I wasn't doing a RHS garden that year, so I decided to pull all the stops out for Mrs Durga. When she returned from Spain, she could not believe how her garden had been transformed. The garden looked perfect for the engagement party and was a great hit with her family and friends.

I had to design a garden in Wimbledon. The client had bought the house next door to his and wanted to claim the bottom half of the garden and add it to his own, giving the other property a smaller garden. This made good sense as the gardens were long and narrow, and now he could open his out so as not to have the 'tunnel' look.

Often, I liked to do my designs on site, and I almost always worked out the timings on site too. I stood in the garden and thought, with pen and paper in hand, what should I do? I immediately had a vision of a curve of a birch tree part-way around a circular lawn. This was the second time I had a vision for a garden. Delighted, I incorporated this into the design, confident that the client would love my design as spirit had given me the overall idea. When the presentation drawing was ready, I arranged to meet with the client. He took one look and said he didn't like it! I was gutted. He wanted me to come up with something else. I was puzzled. Why had I seen this garden, only for the client to not like it? I trusted my vision and was left scratching my head again. There was nothing I could do but come up with a different design, which I duly did, and the client loved.

Some weeks after this, I had an appointment at a new site. This was a smart hotel in the east of the city. Based on my copy of the London A-Z, I read the map and parked up where I thought the place was. There were huge modern blocks of flats with plenty of landscaping. It was a newish development, probably 10-15 years old, by the river, opposite the Millennium Dome. I walked along the river past the blocks of flats, looking for the hotel. I rounded a corner and went up some steps, and there in front of me was the garden I had seen in my vision. It was very simple and based on a curve of birch trees partway around a circular lawn.

It was still not the hotel, however, which turned out to be in the next block along. Now, this vision got my attention! I met the client at the hotel, and she gave me the brief. I was VERY attentive, knowing this appointment was very important. The client kept changing the brief, and you could say she was messing me around. Usually, I would probably have given up, but because of the vision, I jumped through every one of the hoops that the lady put in front of me.

After this job, the client awarded me the contract at another of their hotels and also at the director's private house. His garden was more like a park and even had a lake in it. It was the largest contract I had ever got. I knew then why spirit had given me the vision. I think it was from my grandfather. When he went over to the other side, he could see how hard I worked and wanted to give me a boost. He gave me the vision of the garden to ensure that I gave the client my undivided attention to get the contract.

Snow Vision

I had an office from time to time, as my business slowly grew. It wasn't healthy to have all the paperwork at home. It was hard enough to switch off anyway, and to come home to a front room that doubled as my office certainly did not help.

One office was in an old stable yard in East Sheen. I had a room at the end and up a flight of steps, so there was a view right down the mews-like lane. The other units were rented out to artists, cottage industries and other small businesses. One day in this office, I was at my desk working away, fully concentrating on the task at hand, when I happened to glance up. I blinked and suddenly saw snow falling! It was mid-summer and a warm day. I blinked again and again, repeating it several times, but the snow continued to fall. Then, after another blink, the sky went back to being blue. "We are going to have a very hard winter this year. Spirit was warning me so that I could adjust my business accordingly." I thought.

I decided to book a winter holiday in Australia that year. Sure enough, it was the hardest winter for many years. I told a client so that I had a witness.

"Let's see if your prophecy comes true," she said, before adding, "People sometimes know things."

Hawaiian Paradise

The yoga group had become a good source for social group holidays, and the trips were always filled with lots of laughter. They had started to visit Hawaii each year to whale watch, swim with wild dolphins, along with practising yoga, and there would be a lot of free time. It turned out that the Dr, who I had seen all those years ago when she iridologised my eyes, used to take a group there every year. When her circumstances changed, she handed the baton over to Dianna. Dianna had since become an avid member of the yoga group, so the event became a part of the yoga group's diary.

Dianna was heavily committed to the yoga group and added another dimension to the dolphin trips when the yoga teacher came along to lead the trips and offer some morning and evening yoga.

I decided to join them for a trip to Hawaii, a place I had never been. Once again, this holiday was spectacular. The group had now been many times and knew the ropes, so to speak. We would swim and snorkel in the clear waters, eat the plentiful tropical fruit, go on whale-watching trips, and swim with the dolphins. It really was a paradise.

Unlike the other tourist boats, which are mainly American, we would travel in silence and with an air of reverence and respect. The boat's skipper was asked to turn his radio off, and we would venture out to sea quietly. We saw some spectacular sights of whales breaching. The American law was that a boat was not to approach a whale within 200 meters, but if the whale came up to the boat, that was a different matter.

On this particular day, we had been travelling for some time, and no whales had been sighted. I looked down and hung my head as my mind reflected on London matters. Spotting me, the leader said to keep my chin up. As I lifted my head, a giant whale leapt fully out of the water, seeming to defy gravity as it remained motionless in the air before crashing back down into the sea. It was an awesome sight. Later on that trip, we were treated to a whale calf playing around our boat.

The next day, while on a snorkelling trip, a fisherman beckoned our boat across with hand signals. He kept pointing down into the water, and when he saw that we were making for where he was indicating, he left us to go about his fishing.

After stopping at the location he had pointed, we all jumped into the open sea in our snorkelling gear. Below us, swimming a slow figure of 8, was a fully mature whale shark. Wow, we were so lucky! Before too long, an American tourist charter arrived, complete with music blaring. They joined us in the water, and before you knew it, there were dozens of people swimming with the whale shark, some even getting a free ride by holding on to its fin!

A year or two later, I went with the group to Hawaii again. Dianna had hired the same house for our communal living. Many of the same people were there, and we had great fun again. There were avocados growing just outside our building, which we could pick and eat straight from the tree. After ten days of swimming in the crystal-clear sea, with perfect weather, all that exercise, such wonderful food and no hassles or worries in the world, I felt so relaxed and content.

One day, we went out to sea to spot a whale. It was a dry day, and we were just ready to turn back when the skipper spotted a school of dolphins. He headed in their direction, but they were travelling too fast for us to jump in with them. "I've never seen dolphins so far out to sea," the skipper remarked. Then, as though they had reached a traffic light, the dolphins suddenly took a left turn and started to swim in seemingly random directions.

"Now's your chance," the skipper said, prompting all the swimmers amongst us to jump into the sea. As my head hit the open ocean, I could hear a whale's music. It was so loud! I was looking around the open ocean for the whale, but being the deep sea, I couldn't see far. The singing was wonderful. I had heard whale music on a CD, and it didn't do anything for me; in fact, I had found it really irritating, but to be in the ocean and hear it filling my ears was something else. It was so loud I thought that the whale must be very close by. My whole body buzzed. I searched all around to see if I could spot the whale whose song it was, but with no joy. I grew tired and gave up my quest. It had alluded me. In my concentration, I had broken off from the group. I looked around and caught sight of the boat a way off. I could see the skipper beckoning me, with a wave of his arm, back to the boat.

I put my mask back on and started to flipper back. Behold! There was a whale under the boat! Motionless. It was a young male. Perhaps he thought that the underside of the boat was his mother. I floated in a frog poise, motionless in the water, gasping with elation. I lifted my head out of the water, took out my snorkel and shouted to the skipper. "There's a whale under the boat." Then, I adjusted my apparatus and started to swim towards the whale. In a moment, the whale swam off in the other direction. Those who had remained on the boat saw the whale, too. I was so excited; I felt like the luckiest person in the whole world. I later bragged that I had swam with a whale!

I took the same trip the following year. This time, we didn't see so many whales, but it turned out to be a trip for dolphins. We were with our same scout and went to the now favoured places. At one point, we were in a cove when we were suddenly joined by dozens of dolphins. We jumped in and swam in the clear waters with them. At one point, Dianna and I swam for what seemed like 20 minutes with a dolphin swimming between us! I really think the dolphin was having as much fun as we were.

Later, I amused myself by just floundering around aimlessly before realising I had unintentionally broken off from the main group again. Suddenly, in the depths way below me, I saw a shimmering, glinting shape. I swam closer, and it became clear. Below me was a group of dolphins swimming nose to tail in a perfect circle. There must have been 20 to 30 of these incredible animals. I swam forward to position myself right in the middle of the circle on the sea's surface, marvelling at the sight below of a perfect circle.

A perfect circle of dolphins. These were wild dolphins; this was no circus or zoo trick. I flippered this way and that to stay in the middle of the circle. The dolphins had another source of fun, and the circle started to rise! Wow, I'm going to be surrounded, I realised. They rose up and up, still making a circle around where I swam on the surface. As they approached closer, they broke formation and started to jump into the air and swim in all directions. I was surrounded by this frolicking! I mimicked the dolphins and spun myself around as best I could in my cumbersome way. This went on until I grew tired and could no longer play along. I made my way back to the boat. Again, I felt like the luckiest person alive.

As I climbed back into the boat, the leader shot me a glance. "You have had your fix," she said.

In hindsight, I now know that the circle of dolphins was an answer, a blessing, and an incredible experience. The circle of life comes to mind, a literal one, which I found myself in the very middle of. This was an answer to a question I had put out to the universe in my search for meaning in life, and just as the aborigines had carved in the stones on The Bluff in my hometown, that answer was a circle, the circle of life.

We can put out questions in our mind to God, the universe, and the spiritual dimension, but they won't answer on demand! They will answer when they are ready with divine timing. When they answered me, I didn't even know it until later.

On the last day of the trip, I had a miniature bottle of Cointreau to drink. I set to work and put 12 wine glasses with the rim wetted and then dipped in sugar put into the fridge to chill. I picked oranges and took the skin off the segments. These were sliced up and put into the now chilled glasses with the Cointreau poured over each glass equally. It was a nice treat to celebrate our wonderful trip.

Chapter Eight

LIGHT

Giving readings was my own way of helping people, but it also helped me. I found that if I didn't work spiritually, I would miss it, and after a period of not working, I would feel that my life was empty. I had felt my life's mission was to help out. Spirit work had given me many answers to life's questions, broadened my mind and helped me to see things from a different perspective. So many strange things had happened that I thought it must all be for a reason; there had to be a purpose to it all.

A gardening client had said to me, "He is on a mission, but he doesn't know what his mission is." Nothing could have been further from the truth. To give some comfort from a departed one cannot have any measure put on it.

Monument Valley with 18 Women

One day, I was daydreaming and wondered where the most beautiful part of the world would be. It would be an undiscovered crystal cave, I mused.

Sometime later, another holiday came up with the yoga group. This time, it was to Utah, New Mexico, Arizona, and Colorado and was being organised by two local American girls. The trip was split into two halves, the first being a residential week of yoga, while the second half was when we would travel and discover the wonders these four states had to offer. I had a feeling before I had said anything about my intention to go on the trip that I would be the only male!

Due to work commitments, I wasn't able to take the whole time off and would miss out on the first part altogether before joining the others for the travelling part of the expedition. Of course, I cleared this up with the leader first.

I arrived on the last day of the yoga to find that one young man was only there for the yoga part of the trip before flying back early due to his work commitments! So, at first, he was the only male, and then it was me and 18 women.

On the way to the airport, I suddenly panicked, wondering if I would be mothered or smothered. As it happened, nobody mothered or smothered me one bit, and after a few days of holidaying, I felt that I had never been so relaxed! I felt under no pressure whatsoever to be like this or like that, and I could just be my chilled-out self. I realised that it was being around other males that made me feel competitive and pressurised. A psychologist would have a field day explaining that about myself!

The first trip was to the Navajo reservation land in the spectacular Monument Valley. We had been on a horse ride through the desert monuments of stone and were travelling back in the car to the motel when I realised I had not given back the registration form, which the farm needed for insurance purposes for riding their horses.

I was given the car keys and drove back to the corral. As it was a national park, I had to pass through a checkpoint and at the barrier, I asked the attendant what the name of the nearest rock formation was as I felt drawn to it.

"Mitten," he said, "it's Navajo for hand."

The formation had a separate rock pillar to the side, which looked vaguely like a thumb, making the rest of the mound look like a hand.

I drove on, returned the form to the grateful horseman, and headed back to our motel. The next day, we went to some ancient Navajo land

and scrambled over rocks and through scrubland, ending up beside a large rocky overhang that almost formed a cave. Inside were ancient paintings and hand prints. Our guide spoke to us about these, explaining their origin and meanings.

"Mitten," I said, pointing to one particular set of markings.

"Yes," he replied.

The leader was gobsmacked. "What did you say?" he exclaimed. She thought I was conversing in Navajo with the guide!

The morning that we were due to leave the hot spring resort at Ojo Caliente, I arose early and decided to go for a walk in the hills. I left the hotel grounds and made my way along a track towards the ridge that extended out in front of me. As I headed off, I saw a figure ahead of me climbing up the ridge. Somebody had the same idea as me, and I suddenly realised it was the leader. As her figure disappeared over the ridge of the hill, I found myself hoping she didn't think I was following her.

I reached the brow of the ridge and gazed out over the flat land that stretched out before me. A few hills dotted here, and there broke up the landscape, and in the distance was a more prominent, pudding-shaped hill with a dusting of snow. I could see the leader in the distance, now just a tiny speck.

I carried on walking, occasionally catching a glimpse of the moving speck in front of me. The path divided several times, and I ended up following my nose and heading in the general direction of the pudding-shaped mountain. I had walked for some time, and if it hadn't been for the knowledge that the leader was somewhere out in front, I would have turned back. The weather started to change and closed in, and light flurries of snowflakes began to fall. I continued on my way regardless, with the snow getting heavier and thicker until it carpeted the ground. Everywhere became silent, the way it does when there is a snowfall.

There came a point when I realised that the leader was no longer in front of me, and I knew that I had better run back shortly. I wanted to go a little further first, however, as by now, I had reached the pudding-shaped mountain, and the track was starting to descend. At the spa complex, they had said that there was a mica mine in the hills, and I was intrigued to see if I could see any.

I came round a bend in the rocks and, for the second time in my life, saw three caves. They were just off the path, cut into a ridge. "Ahh, I must have found the mica mines," I thought to myself, heading off the path and walking up to the caves.

It turned out that the first one was little more than a niche. The mica was like a series of natural mirrors, varying in size, studding the wall. Alongside was quartz crystal, which was held together with clay. I went on to the second cave, which was just four feet deep. The third cave was much deeper, and I walked in.

I turned around and marvelled. All was pure white as the snow fell, and the mica and crystal glimmered and glistened. It was magical. I drew a breath. I'm in a crystal cave, I thought. The soft snow quietly falling outside seemed to shine daylight onto the pieces of mirror-like mica and lighting the quartz: I was in heaven. I remembered imagining the most beautiful place on earth would be a crystal cave! It's ironic that this was man-made, I thought.

Towards the end of the trip, we went on a picnic down a canyon. We had been given the opportunity to opt for a horse ride either one or both ways, or we could go by wagon. I had paid for a horse one way and the wagon on the way back. At the start point, I was handed a magnificent steed. I had only ridden a horse twice before in my life. It was more like holding on rather than riding. This horse was acutely sensitive, and anybody who sat in the saddle looked like an Olympian! At one point, I must have hit the wrong button as the horse started to do dressage as we clipped across the shallow waters of the canyon floor!

High cliffs rose on each side as we journeyed on. It was like something out of an old Wild West film. After a mile or so, the land widened out to some Navajo farmland, and we observed a native woman farmer, one of the last of her people to live some of the old ways. We rode on until we reached some flat rocks on a bend in the river, where we were to have our lunch. We tethered our horses, and I said goodbye to my trusty steed.

After lunch, I was standing on a flat rock when I noticed something by my knee. A bumble bee, I thought, but then, as I looked down, I couldn't help but gasp and marvel at the sight right by me. It was a hummingbird hovering!

"Dianna, look, look!" I cried, pointing to my knee. The bird hovered a moment longer, then darted off. "Did you see that?" I exclaimed. It was actually no bigger than a bumble bee.

With lunch over, it was time to set off back. Elisa had a terrible time controlling her horse on the way down and offered me her steed as she had paid for both ways. Delighted, I accepted her kind offer. I had a marvellous ride. It was a bit more of a 'hang on' ride, but with the horse's nose pointed towards home, he didn't need much encouragement. It was another seamless holiday.

Miracles

After a hard day at work, I was sat in my van on a hill in Golders Green in North London. The sky was full of dark clouds, and the light was beginning to dim. I was deep in thought.

"I know what a miracle is," I thought, recalling the numerous strange experiences I had lived through. "It is being in the right place at the right time when a natural event runs in parallel with a person's experiences."

As that thought was going through my head, the clouds opened up in the sky, and the sun shone down, lighting only me and the van I was sitting in like the beam from a torch! Everywhere else remaining in shadow. I looked around to see if anyone was looking, but the street was quiet and empty. I had a spiritual friend who said that in his childhood, he had an experience where it was only snowing about him. I remembered the theory that I had heard that the volcano at Santorini had erupted at the exact same time that Moses wanted to cross the sea, causing the sea to recede at that very moment, only to then rush back and drown the approaching Egyptian soldiers. This was the same kind of thing, the miracle of synchronicity.

A Few Readings

I hadn't been working spiritually for some time and was missing it. Sitting alone in my kitchen, I thought to myself, "Send your thoughts up to spirit and see what they have to say."

I put my mind in the right place and immediately saw a blue and white plate.

"What are spirit telling me?" I thought. I googled 'blue and white plate', and many images came up. The plate in the middle image was the same Spode one that Kate had given me all those years ago. That was her way of saying she was around me.

A lot of people, when they get to the other side, can see how they have treated others. I believe they can witness the ramifications of their behaviour that they couldn't see from earth's side or chose to ignore at the time. Facing things helps people to see things as they truly are and perhaps learn a better way to behave. The Eastern mystics would call this karma. Plenty of spirit people have come through to offer an apology to one still here. This can be very healing for both parties and helps people grow and move on.

Sometimes, the way spirit interacts is not always obvious. At a Sunday service, I was with a lady and had linked to a spirit that wanted to tell her they would be around her at Christmas time. A few months later, in the spring, I was back at the same church and saw this same lady again. Remembering her reading, I asked if she had felt spirit around her at Christmas.

"No," she said flatly.

Spirit immediately gave me some evidence to support their original claim. "You got a Christmas card from Adam," I said, and she agreed.

"See," I said, "spirit were around you at Christmas, as they know who sent you a Christmas card!"

"I know you were near a mine in Wales," I said. "I'm getting slag heaps and a connection to the slag heap disaster."

"I used to play on the slag heaps as a girl," the lady replied.

The next day on the television, I saw that there was a special garden opening in Wales to commemorate the Aberfan disaster, which killed 144 people in October 1966, 116 of them children.

For another person, I heard the air raid sirens of World War Two in London.

"You are Londoners", I said, and the lady agreed. "I can hear the sirens, so I know there are war stories in your family. A bomb went off very close. I saw the windows blown out."

"Yes," she said, "my father was blown out of his bed by a bomb."

There are times when the messages are less dramatic. A funny one I remember was that spirit showed me a memory of a singer sewing machine. Yes, he could understand that. I went back to spirit and asked why they had shown me that image.

"There was some sewing to do, a broken zip." We all laughed, thinking it was a trouser zip and a few buttons. Then they talked about the ironing: he wasn't doing that either, causing the whole room to burst into laughter once again, poking fun at his dishevelled state.

Hummingbird

I came across a hummingbird card that I had bought on my trip to America with the 18 women. It was my older sister's birthday, so I thought I would send it. It arrived safely, and when I called her the day before her birthday, she thanked me for it. On the day of her birthday, I was going to Richmond Spiritualist Church for a service. I had just looked at a photo album of the trip to America and was thinking of the hummingbird. I arrived at the church and sat down in the medium's chair, ready for the service. I noticed that the water jug on my table had an etching of a hummingbird on it.

I gave my address and told the story of how a hummingbird had hovered by my knee, that I had bought a card all those years ago and had just posted it to my sister for her birthday, which was today, and now I am sitting here, and there is an etching of one in front of me. A sign from the spirit world, I exclaimed. There was a latecomer to the service. After being told about the address, she exclaimed that she had dropped and broken a glass figure of a hummingbird earlier that day. I suggested to the lady that she use the hummingbird as an animal totem!

Clapham Spiritualist Church

I hadn't served Clapham Church for some years as they had stopped booking me when they had undergone a change of committee. I wasn't sure why, as I always worked well there, or at least so I had thought, so I had just left it. Some four or five years later, I got a call out of the blue from them, and they gave me some more bookings.

"What time does the demonstration start?" I asked.

"It isn't a demonstration; it is one-to-ones," the lady replied.

I had just been thinking about how I would like to do one-to-ones again, and it was at Clapham that I gained much of my previous one-to-one experience.

The church itself was in an old rag school. One had to walk through an archway and down a Yorkstone covered alleyway, through a gothic door into a single large room with a small extension for a kitchen. Another door led out to an outdoor toilet. The large room had the usual array of faded fake flowers, which seemed to grace most spiritual churches. I shouldn't mock the artificial blooms as spirit in the past had used them as a point of focus for a name or colour or a drawing me to them to say where they were in a recipient's house!

I had to be there at 6pm on the designated Tuesday and was to give 15-minute readings back-to-back for two hours, eight readings in all. One-to-one readings are great practice as it is not a case of simply going to the most spiritually open person to give a reading to a group of people.

For reasons unknown to me, there were many Portuguese people there that night. I read for three Portuguese first, then an English woman, a Spanish guy, and a German lass before finishing with a Scot, so only seven. The first two were heavy going; all I remember was asking who it was that liked cheese on toast; the lady laughed and said her son. The English woman had mental health problems and was quite aggressive, so I was very careful what I said. She wanted to know where she had lost her mobile phone three weeks before. I thought that was weird as I had lost my mobile phone at Covent Garden Market that very morning when it had slipped out of my pocket as I bent down to inspect a tray of flowers. She was also worried that an aunt had asked if she was pregnant as she had started to put on some weight and wanted to know about any repercussions from the tittle-tattle.

I started to despair that I had lost it when the next sitter came in. Spirit came through with some extraordinary detail from somebody in the spirit world who used to tickle my new sitter. This was clairsentient, so I had an overriding sensation to tickle this complete stranger. I resisted, thank God! Spirit said he was taking life too seriously, and they remembered when he was a child and used to be tickled all the time. Later in the sitting, I said that he had a connection to Lourdes.

"Yes, I do know a Lord of the Manor," came his reply.

"No," I corrected him, "I mean Lourdes in France."

He admitted to having a fascination with sightings of the Holy Mother, which, of course, the whole healing sanctuary at Lourdes is built around. Next was an angelic young woman called Anchora. Her great-grandmother came through beautifully, steadily, and gently with a quiet assurance and showed me my own grandmother on my father's side. Spirit showed me things about my own grandmother, which I repeated, and she accepted it all. Anchora's great-grandmother was very short and had mobility problems as she got older. Her husband had died years earlier, so she had a good period that she spent on her own. She was quiet and gentle, creative, and good with her hands. She spoke of Frau's creative writing, which Frau agreed with. The reading continued until, at the end, I asked if there were any questions.

"Yes," she said innocently and endearingly asked if she should continue to wait for another.

"Romantically?" I asked.

She was a little embarrassed and lowered her eyes as she said yes. I sensed how genuine she was. Some fool was about to seriously lose out. Though my instincts said she should move on, I had to remain professional.

"I can't influence you," I said.

"You must make the decision. I will ask spirit," I went on, not wanting the responsibility of influencing a complete stranger.

I went up to her grandmother, and with that quiet assurance and steady demeanour, she said, "You have been doing some creative writing."

"Yes," the girl said.

"Well, the answer is there already. You have written it already," I said.

"Yes," Anchora said, emphatically agreeing.

This gave me permission to speak out, so I then said that I had thought as soon as she had mentioned it that she should not wait for this fellow.

After the reading, the girl told me that she wrote letters to her deceased grandmother as though she were still alive and put the letters into a box. She had just written a letter and said she would not wait any longer or hold her heart and her life back for this chap!

Evidence with Dates

I had just delivered my work caravan to its parking space near Banbury. In the dedicated caravan car park, there was also a Romany caravan. Later, at a service in a church, spirit showed me that the woman had also seen a Romany caravan unexpectedly. They showed it to me by putting the recent memory I had seen back into the forefront of my mind.

These 'party tricks,' as I sometimes called them, continued. These were pieces of information that were put across in a playful manner, and though evidential, they didn't have any real deep meaning as far as I could make out. Spirit started to give anniversaries next to well-known dates. It was not unusual to say, "You have an anniversary close to Christmas Day."

"Yes."

"Close to Easter."

"Yes."

"Close to Halloween."

"Yes."

"Close to Remembrance Sunday."

"Yes."

Then, it was a play on names.

"Bill."

"Yes."

"Ben."

"Yes." Bill and Ben.

"Mary."

"Yes."

"Joseph."

"Yes," Mary and Joseph. There was also Adam and Eve, April, May and June. I wondered what was coming next!

Speaking about people who had died could sometimes seem morose, so to bring some humour in was a good thing. All that passing on what had finished them off got a bit much sometimes. Julie had said years ago, "Once you get into this, you will never meet another normal person again!" There was certainly some truth in that. The amount of times I observed myself in a demonstration and thought, "I would never have believed I was going to do this! It isn't me." But I carried on.

More Kangaroos

I was working in Mrs Durga's garden when I saw a kangaroo out of the corner of my eye. I immediately turned to look, but it was gone. I took note. "How strange," I thought.

About a fortnight later, the same thing happened in another garden and again, a third time. Then, one evening, as I was putting the key into my front door, I noticed a tiny square of paper on the pavement, only four feet from my door. I bent down and picked it up. Turning it over, it was a child's sticker... of a kangaroo!

I opened the door, went inside and stamped my foot. "I am NOT going back to Australia," I said aloud, realising what the spirit nudges were about.

As I had sacrificed so much to build up my business, I didn't want to go back. I liked my life in the UK. With hindsight, I think this was a nudge to visit.

The Wonderful & Varied World of Mediumship

One of the wonderful things about mediumship is that every time you work, it is different. At Wimbledon, a man came through wearing his vest. I had already identified him to the recipient, so I asked if this man had ever been known to wear only a vest.

"Well, it has been known," he said.

I went back to the man in spirit and asked him why he was showing himself to me like that.

"It's my time off," came the reply. "When I don't have to be anybody or anything to anyone."

I turned back to the recipient. "You need some time off," I told him. "Time where it's just you and your wife, nobody else."

"We were just talking about that," he said.

That evening, whenever a man appeared in the spirit world, he appeared in a vest. They were no doubt telling me the same thing.

A few months earlier, I had done a 'psychic supper' at Hackbridge Spiritualist Church, a sister church to Wimbledon. At a 'psychic supper,' a medium sits at each table and gives everyone a reading as they eat their meal. Hazel Robinson was there and sat at my table. Spirit gave her various bits of information, including "Your next birthday is a biggie."

"Yes, I'm 80," she said. Spirit then said that a surprise birthday was being planned, and I gave her a cheeky wink. She smiled knowingly back. Also there that evening were her son and daughter-in-law, and spirit said, "A big celebration is coming up?"

"Yes," she said, but the son and his wife knew nothing about it. I had to laugh, as the ones getting the surprise were the children. I hadn't spoilt it because spirit had told me. They would only have done that if the woman had already worked it out for herself.

Then, spirit went to a young girl. A woman came forward and described herself, and the girl immediately knew who it was. The woman gave a lot of clear evidence, all of which the girl could take. The girl smiled at me as I delivered the information. The lady in the spirit world was very emotional, and I had to hold back the tears. Later in the message, she came back with all the emotion again.

"Why are you so emotional?" I asked. I explained how she missed the girl, how much love and pride there was for her, and also that she wanted to give her a big hug. Her answer surprised me. The woman was stunned that she could communicate with her niece. She had thought that when she died, that was to be it. She was shocked to the back teeth that life carried on and was so glad she could watch all those she loved. I relayed all this to the girl. Nobody in spirit had told me that before. She got the surprise of her "life" after she had died!

A few days later, the same church texted me to ask if I would do their Sunday service. I thought it would be a damp squib, but it couldn't have been further from the truth. The energy was amazing, and I was flying.

I went to a lady and delivered what I could; then, as I was about to leave her, a man rushed forward.

"I betted." He said, and she accepted him immediately just off that.

"I took a gamble," he carried on, "and I'm gambling on you; you're a sure bet, 14," he said.

I repeated what I had heard, saying it was either a house number or the date of an anniversary.

"Both." The lady said.

Spirit wrapped angel wings around her and then said, "You have seen a feather, a real one, drop in front of you."

"Yes."

I don't usually talk in this language of angels, but this lady understood, so I passed it on.

Earlier, I read to a woman with two spinster aunts who had been very religious. They came through, and at first, I had a wordplay and joked she knew a Bill and a Ben, an Adam and an Eve, a Mary and a Joseph! They had played this joke to me before. Spirit stopped me.

"Who in this room knows a Jesus!"

A Spaniard spoke out. There we are: Mary, Joseph and Jesus. It sounded irreverent, but perhaps the energy needed lifting with some humour.

The following Wednesday, I was working at Richmond for their evening of clairvoyance. There can't have been more than eight people there. I started with some information. I didn't have a clue where I was going. A few people accepted the information. I kept delivering more information until only one person accepted what was coming through.

When I finally got to one person, I said, "It's a knockout." When it finally comes down to one person, I feel that I can settle down and give the message in hand.

I had been told by a medium that spirit would work with me differently. I wondered if tonight was that night. I asked spirit for more information. Immediately, they showed me Rapunzel in a tower. Well, that was certainly different. I went into the image again with my mind and got some feeling with it.

This helped me interpret the image. Without feeling, it is easy to misinterpret a symbol. The lady accepted my interpretation and even accepted somebody with extremely long hair.

"Yes, I'm working differently," I thought.

In the second reading, a man came through and said he fought in the Far East and served in a prisoner-of-war camp in the Second World War. The lady recipient corrected me and said her father had fought in the First World War in the Far East, and her brother was in a prisoner-of-war camp. I had bunched the two together. This lady came up to me later and told me how much she had needed the message.

"I'm nearly 80," she informed me. You wouldn't have known.

"You've had a rough life. They said some people were not nice to you, and you deserve an apology."

"Yes," she said.

A man came forward and apologised to this lady.

"People thought you would crumple, but you never did. You held your chin up and kept your cool. People were so surprised, and you proved many people wrong." Spirit then said, "You could write a book."

The lady replied it was the second time she had been told that week.

The message continued, "It's because you can help people. What you have been through will help others. Also, it will be like a manual, and people won't need to go through so much if they have read your book. They will know what to do and stop in their tracks."

Tears began to roll down the old lady's lined face. Spirit showed me a mirror. It had three sections to it and was on a mantelpiece. I relayed this information, and she told me she understood where it was. I saw her looking into the mirror and knew she felt connected to the two worlds. As sometimes is the case, I didn't know what I was saying or why I was saying it, but it was one of those messages that was word for word.

I was in Clapham Spiritualist Church and had a link with the chairlady. Two very religious aunts had come through and had rolled the round tombstone open from Jesus' tomb. They then turned the stone into a cake. I knew instantly that they would bake a round cake, especially for Easter. These were Italians. Yes, the woman confirmed, they used to do that.

About a year later, I was at Kingston Market, where they have a very good French bread stall that is always stacked with all sorts of delicious loaves and pastries. This time, I noticed some round pastries with a handwritten sign propped up next to them. I started to read. It was the 6th of February, and every year, the French celebrate when the three wise men visited Jesus with a round pastry. Remembering the Italian story of the round Easter cake, I bought one just for fun.

Shortly after, I was back at Clapham Church, and the same chairlady was there. Lo and behold, the two aunts came through for her again. This time, they talked about cakes they baked for a festival but had a hole in them.

"Yes," the chair lady said. Immediately, they gave me the significance.

"Sometimes you feel something is missing, that you are not perfect. But you are perfect," spirit continued.

It might sound corny, but it is absolutely correct. Seeds of self-doubt are present in many people, but we are all perfect!

War Stories

I had to go to Holland to look at trees. I was met at the airport, and we went to the nursery and spent the day viewing trees. For lunch, I was taken to the local village. We sat down at a restaurant, but it was not open, so we headed to another one down the road. As we tucked into some traditional Dutch fare, we noticed a file of people walking past and over the road to the closed restaurant. It was a wake. The mourners had booked out the restaurant. My tree man started to talk about his father, who had passed away a year earlier. As he spoke, I thought, "I'm supposed to be a medium, yet I can't feel his dad around him."

"What did he do for a living?" I asked.

"He had a greenhouse."

I knew immediately that he grew tomatoes.

"He grew tomatoes," the tree man said. I didn't think it was appropriate to make a connection, especially as his dad wasn't coming forward and hitting me with information. I listened to him talk about his father, and we had a lovely meal before returning to work.

At the end of the day, he had to take me back to the airport, saying he would go the scenic route as the motorway would be jammed. We headed off, driving through some attractive countryside and over a canal or two. Suddenly, I had an overpowering feeling about the war.

"What happened here during the war," I asked. "I can feel it."

My host started to tell me that his father had told of how his family had hidden a Jewish family for a week, and his mother's family had hidden people for three months. Moments later, he pointed out his father's old house and greenhouse. Now I felt him around me. He wanted to tell his son that he loved him and was sorry that he didn't show him more emotion when he was alive. The tree man was such a nice guy.

A week later, I had to serve at a spiritual church in Finchley. Just before the service, I felt a strong spiritual presence, so I knew I was topped up for the clairvoyance ahead. I went to the first recipient, and the messages were loud and strong for her. I was shown a brown picture of a man in the Air Force sporting a moustache.

"Yes," she said.

I went back to spirit.

"There were jokes with him about Hitler," I said, referring to his moustache.

"Yes," she said, "plenty."

I went back to spirit again, and they said that a joke had been made recently, and a person found the joke insulting and got upset. They did not realise that it was meant just as a joke. I relayed this, and again, I got a positive response. Spirit told me that when she calms down, I should reassure her that it was only meant as a joke. She had cause to be offended, but the words were not meant to offend.

Spirit came through with lots of things for this lady, peculiar evidence such as that she had a conch shell facing up on her table and a nautilus shell, that she had memories of donkey rides on the beach and had given money to a donkey sanctuary,, that she could take the name of Mary, and that she could take the name of Joseph.

What is this? I said, "Mary, Joseph, and a donkey?" Spirit were having another laugh, but we weren't being irreverent.

I noticed that I would often get the name of Shirley in a reading for others. Hardly a demonstration would go by without me getting this name. This went on for many months, perhaps even a year. The name was always accepted, but as it was repeated so often, I realised that it was someone whom I would meet who would be important to me. My best friend from school's mum's name was Shirley, as was a lovely lady at Wimbledon Church, but I knew neither of these was the person being mentioned.

The name had long stopped coming up, but I eventually met a lady with that name who was a huge help. She did phone readings for me, which were always very positive when I felt particularly downtrodden at work. By then, the gardening business had been built up to a decent size, and I didn't always have all the bases covered. She was such a help. She repeatedly reminded me that if I wasn't feeling right, I was picking up something from someone else. All the spirit work I was doing only increased my empathy to a point where it seemed difficult not to pick up another's energy unconsciously. I remembered Sharry constantly hammering home to us to close down! One would think that being a medium, one would have all the answers. Actually, I think that we do hold all our own answers, but when one is busy in life and distracted, it is nice to turn to another for some help.

Shirley made me laugh one day, telling me how, on an occasion, when someone went to her door for a reading, she was told that she looked normal! I am normal she answered. That was precisely how I felt when I first met Julie! Mediums are very normal, just what we do is not mainstream.

Chapter Nine

LIFE LESSONS

My personal life had suffered with all my focus and energies being directed into building my business up and my dedication to spiritual work. Earlier relationships had led me to throw myself into work, and I stopped looking for someone.

I sent a thought up to God that I wouldn't look anymore, and if I was meant to be with somebody, God would have to send them. Well, you know what they say, be careful what you wish for! About the very next day, some people came to look at the flat as prospective lodgers. It was love at first sight. I never got to touch this person, and I had my heart broken. It took me three years to get over it until finally, I heard my grandmother in the spirit world say, "Why don't you build a shrine!" This was the kick I needed; finally, the chord was broken, and I healed. We must have had a past life connection. I had also asked God if I had any karma to work through, please give it to me so I could work through it and then move on with no nasty surprises. Again, be careful what you wish for because several things came along that nearly flattened me!

Friends

I thought fondly of my friends in Kent. Kate was like a sister and looked out for me. One day, I had a dream from her that a baby girl would be born into the family. As it happened, the day after I had this dream, I was seeing her daughter for dinner. When we met, I told her immediately.

About eight months later, I heard that she was pregnant, and of course, I knew she had a girl. She was born three weeks early, and I met her on her due date. It was very special as I considered myself an honorary uncle.

Dreams come through with various qualities, and sometimes, it is obvious that they come from the spirit world. Other times, the dream may be a bit jumbled, making it hard to fathom if it is just the unconscious mind processing the day's rabble or if it is indeed spirit. I found that when emotions came with the dream, it was an indicator of spirit's influence. I had many dreams that would wake me up in the night.

I had a gardening client, The Jonas. I worked for them for at least 20 years. They were a very close couple, and Amelia had a hard grieving process to go through when Dennis passed a long time before her. One night, I woke up with a dream fresh in my mind. I had dreamt of the Jonas family, the whole family, the children and their children. I had heard one word loudly, uttering the word "Venice." I called Amelia the next day and said I hoped she didn't mind me talking to her in this way, and I relayed the dream exactly. She burst out laughing. Apparently, it was a family joke that Dennis would take her to Venice before they were married. This was in the days when courting couples were chaperoned everywhere. "You have made my day," she said. Dennis had a great sense of humour.

I relayed a story to the class that had happened a month earlier. A chap looked after some gardens for me in the Cotswolds. He did this on his days off from his day job in the hospitality industry. He couldn't visit any of the gardens in December due to the Christmas parties, and in January, he returned to his home country. This left me to look after the gardens and put them to bed for the winter. I arranged a couple of trips, which involved staying overnight.

The hotel we stayed in came with an ensuite leading off from my bedroom. The day had been cold and wet, so I decided to have a nice hot soak in the bath, especially as in my home in London, the hot water never came out hot enough for a bath, so my bathing days were over, having to resort to showers. A bath had become a great treat.

As it fell dark by 4.30, we had long evenings to fill. Chilled and damp, a nice hot bath seemed the perfect thing to do. I squirted the hotel tube of bubbles into the steaming bath and lowered myself in for a good soak! Ahh, I was in heaven, now and then topping up the hot water with my toes on the taps.

The phone pinged as a text message arrived. I leaned over and looked. It read, "Hello, about the bath." I wasn't sure who the message was from; I looked around. Is this some kind of joke? "I would like it vertical, not horizontal, under the window!" I looked at previous messages and realised it had been sent by accident by Jonas's daughter, who is an interior designer, thinking she was sending it to her builder. Knowing how spirit works, I knew they were having a joke with me!

Another time Amelia asked me to do some extra work, it was on the weekend, and I texted her to ask if I should proceed. "Go ahead" came back the text. I went to reply. I had a strong urge to answer with my Kentish name, which the Jonas's didn't know me by. I texted back, "Thanks, James." It turned out that Amelia's grandson was playing with her phone. He had sent the message. His name was James. And when I texted back, "Thanks, James," they thought I must be in the same restaurant where they were having a family meal. They even looked around, searching for me.

Another time, I wondered if my old boss, Mike Miller, from the Harrods of garden centres, was ever around me in the spirit world. Very clearly and almost immediately, I had a dream of his cousin, now my client, and I heard the words "Michael Winner." I Googled the celebrity and saw a striking resemblance between him and my client. "Yes, I was teased about that once I went grey," he told me. "We have a great resemblance." Yet again, I had my proof.

Del Boy in the Afterlife

When I first started out as a working medium, Wimbledon Spiritualist Church would book me all of the time. It was run by a pioneer of the modern-day spirit world movement, Derek Robinson. He had managed some great names from back in the day, including Doris Stokes. Also, he organised the first spirit cruises, as well as a revival of psychic suppers and residential spiritual courses away. What I liked about him was that he was just so passionate and dedicated about the spiritual movement.

At his funeral, I fully realised how much this man was loved and respected. His funeral was a real celebration of his life. When my mother later died, I was determined to organise her funeral on the same slant as a happy celebration of her life rather than a mourning.

Sometime after he had passed, I thought to myself, if anybody knows what it is like on the other side of life, Derek would. A few days later, I was driving along the motorway and just getting onto the exit slip road when Derek came to me. Of all the places to be!

"It's very multidimensional over here," was all he said, answering my question. It was just like in the Bible reading, "God's house has many mansions."

Derek communicated with me directly several times after he passed. Later, he came through to his son and separately to his grandson, both spiritualists, carrying the baton on with his spiritualist beliefs. Ray and his wife Jackie were spiritualist ministers, and their son was a medium. Derek really helped me with my mediumship, believing in me and letting me work so often at his church. I became friends with his wife, Hazel, too. Like her husband, Hazel also came through with messages after she had passed over.

Derek's nickname was Del Boy, which was exactly what his character was like. Just before going out, he would slap me on the back and say something like, "Go sock it to them, boy!" He meant very well, and I felt like a boxer going into the ring. I knew that he believed in me and my mediumship. I needed someone like that, so I took every demonstration or service he gave me.

Sheepskin Rug & Potato Stamp

I had a weekday evening of clairvoyance at Hornsey in North London. As it wasn't a Sunday church service, more people attended. I had a decent number of people there, including a few regular people off the street, not the usual churchgoers. I liked this as I thought I would be able to give messages to people who didn't normally receive them. I felt that I was more likely to help someone. I linked to a lady in the congregation who had gypsy blood. Her grandfather was a great communicator, and the lady took all of the information.

In a few demonstrations, I noticed that spirit had given me a sheepskin rug. The recipient could always accept that they used to have one or still had one. I never questioned spirit why they were telling me this but just assumed it was for a piece of evidence. This time, I had a gypsy in spirit who had lived the traditional ways. The sheepskin rug was mentioned, and this time, spirit went another step further; the sheepskin rug was to put newborn babies on.

It may seem a small thing, but I was amazed that spirit was telling me something I didn't know before. Spirit talk about things that they can retrieve from my memory banks, my filing cabinet if you like, but this piece of information was not in my filing cabinet, so I was thrilled they could extend what I knew. They did the same with the potato stamp, which I had never done or learned about as a child. So when they showed me a potato from spirit side, I had to think, "What on earth are they telling me such a thing?" I had to wait for them to tell me the next thing before it all made sense. They then cut the potato in half, and as I repeated it aloud, they cut the stamp into the potato! The recipient had a childhood memory of this, and that was spirit's way of saying "Yes "to something the recipient had asked the spirit people in their prayers. It was a stamp of approval, albeit a potatoe stamp!

Morocco

The final trip that I went on with the yoga group was to a riad in Marrakesh, Morocco. Originally planned as a yoga weekend, four of us, old travelling companions from our previous excursions, decided to go out a week earlier, with the four of us splitting into two groups. David and Daniel decided upon a beach holiday in Essaouira, while Dianna and I opted for a car hire and an adventure in the mountains before meeting back up for the organised weekend of yoga.

As the plane made its descent into Marrakesh airport, Dianna, the lady with whom I had swam with the dolphins and the one who had taken on Dr's mantle of dolphin swimming in Hawaii, suddenly said that she had changed her mind and would be beaching it with David and Daniel! Talk about last minute!

I was gutted but stuck to my guns. I resolved to hire a car and be adventurous all on my own, leaving Dianna with the now 3 D's for their beach holiday. I brushed it aside, hired the car, and set off for the mountains.

It wasn't long before a local motorbike rider offered to chaperone me onto the right highway, all done through my open window as we shouted to each other as we drove along! When the motorcyclist got me as far as he could go, he waved me onto the highway before dropping away.

That biker was very demonstrative of the people of Morocco. Often, they would say to me that they were "rich in heart", touching their chest as they said it. This was also a silent way of saying they were "poor in pocket." Living in a 'McDonald's world' where money and mass production are king and God, these people were so endearing that they really were rich in heart and had a great generosity of spirit and warmth.

Morocco was what I thought Israel would be like. Most of the people lived the old ways, and it was like going back in time a thousand or so years! People lived in mud houses, and horses or donkeys pulling a cart were not uncommon sight, nor was a beast pulling a plough through the fields.

The Atlas Mountain loomed up in the distance. Generally speaking, I headed for it and went around its left side. Eventually, there was a decision to make: whether to go down the Dades valley or another that forked off in a different direction. I chose the Dades. I stopped at a few towns along the way and eventually reached the Sahara Desert! Here, I did the tourist thing and slept the night under the stars, followed by the obligatory camel ride the following morning.

Travelling back, I drove the other way around the mountain. During breakfast at one particular hotel, I pocketed a couple of small bread rolls I planned to eat later. As lunchtime arrived, my tummy rumbled, and I thought, "I need a filling for my bread rolls." I rounded a turn in the road, now climbing around the mountain, and there in the middle of the road, no more than a second after my thought, there, once again, was a tomato! In this desolate land, it was even more unlikely to see such a thing! I pulled over, washed the bright red fruit down with my bottle of water, and had it in my bread roll.

Several hours later, I arrived back in Marrakesh; I returned my car hire and made my way to the riad. Marrakesh is a fantastic city. The souk market is amazing, with its labyrinths of paths winding their way past the numerous stalls. As one ventured around the city, there were so many workshops where a family would make their living by producing their own speciality and eeking out their livelihood.

Back in the riad, I donned my, at the time, favourite T-shirt, which was in the Brazilian country's colours of green and yellow. The yellow wording said, along with a motif, "ping pong club." The leader and her partner commented on it, words that didn't make sense.

"What?" I asked.

"Ping pong club," they replied.

It turned out they had formed a group called the 'ping-pong club!' Again, a coincidence; I felt qualified! And unknowingly, I wore a T-shirt with that name.

When I boarded the plane in Morocco to fly back to London, I had a similar experience to when I sat in a circle, and the energy of a tiger surrounded me. As strange as it may sound, I buckled my belt and relaxed, and there was the energy of an elephant with me! It was so real that I felt like I could reach out and touch it. Where did I connect with an elephant, I thought?

Spiritual Junkies & Keeping One's Feet on the Ground

When people first immerse themselves in alternative things, it is quite common to try everything on the menu. As everything is so new to the beginner, people are not sure at first where their own particular path lies. For some people, it was healing. This in itself could fork off into many facets: spiritual healing, laying on hands, reiki, colour healing, crystal healing, animal healing, homeopathy, and herbalism, to name just a few.

With readings, there were psychic readings, tarot card readings, rune readings, palmistry, trance readings, sand reading, flower reading, astrology, past life readings, guide readings, psychic art and mediumship. When I was at the college, I had a taster of many different things, but it was mediumship and 'hands-off' healing that always interested me.

The College of Psychic Studies also held lectures on topics ranging from aliens to a global shift in consciousness.

I liked mediumship mainly because of the evidence. It was factual, and its aim was to help people, to give them a firm handrail to hold onto, as opposed to the somewhat obscure energy healing, where any ache or twinge means you may be 'processing' something. Otherwise, one could go along one's whole life looking for answers when they were right in front of you, and in a way, we all have our own answers within us anyway.

When You Touch the Angel, He Feels You

The years seemed to disappear, and the readings generally got stronger as time went by. I thought to myself how far things had gone from my first attempt at linking with spirit all those years ago when I had seen a yacht sink, and that was all.

I was at Richmond Spiritualist Church taking their Sunday service. There were around 15 people there. The service proceeded as usual, in the typical format of an opening prayer, a healing prayer, reading, address and then the clairvoyance. Richmond always had a lovely atmosphere, making it easier to work.

A man came through and said specifically that he was a traveller, and his job was tarmacking and laying kerbs, a typical profession for travellers, I gather. A girl in the front row immediately said yes. He gave a variety of information all of which she could accept without hesitation, even having spent time in prison. Then I thought he said the name Angela.

"You can understand the name of Angela," I asked.

"No," she said.

I went back to him and got the message, "You're my angel," which I relayed to the girl and asked her if she could understand him saying that.

"Oh yes, "she replied.

"Now I'm your angel," he went on. Clairvoyantly I then clearly saw a statue of an angel.

"In your house, you have the statue of an angel," I said.

"Yes," was her emotional reply.

"When you touch the angel, he feels you," I relayed.

"Yes," she said again, now in tears.

Then, the man did something no spirit has done before or since. He turned, shook my hand, looked me in the eye, and said, "Thank you!" I felt him shake my hand so clearly in my mind. When he turned and looked at me, I felt as though he was looking right through my soul! NO spirit person had thanked me before. The man was a real gentleman and very polite. This was part of the message. Although he had been on the wrong side of the law, he still had a great courtesy about him. The girl came up to me afterwards and said that her father had passed quickly in hospital after a short illness. In hospital, he had the figurine of an angel with him, and he had entrusted it to his daughter just before passing away. Every night, as she went to bed, she kissed the angel.

"When you touch the angel, he feels you." He was saying that he felt her every kiss.

PART TWO

To My Mother, Enid Grace Hewitt, nee Sanders.

Trip to 3 Hummock Island

We left Devonport on Good Friday, picking up 10 people along the coast, arriving at Wyayard airport for our 35 minute flight to Three Hummock Island. The Island lies 50 km North West of Smithton and is part of the Hunter Group. We set off in 2 Cessnas, one fairly old and the other newer and faster. The day was glorious and we had marvelous views along the coast, The Sisters Hills had been devastated by fire earlier in the year and was black, bare and burnt to the shoreline.

We arrived safely at the Island and landed on a grass airstrip. A battered 4 wheel drive was waiting to transport us to our accommodation and a tractor and trailer for our luggage.

We enjoyed a lovely morning tea, then visited the wharf area. A huge Conga eel lives under the jetty and came out to feed from scraps of fish thrown into the water. A very big star fish was lurking there and shoals of little fish. Dinner consisted of freshly caught fish and fruit.

In the afternoon all 10 of us and Rob Alliston the driver, piled into the 4 wheel drive and toured the southern end of the Island. The country is fairly open, with low scrub, tussocks and sandy soils. Marrum grass has been planted to hold the soil together. There were lots of Forrester Kangaroos, Cape Barren Geese and a few sheep. We saw a wedge tailed Eagle circling in the sky. The bird life is plentiful and similar to that of Tasmania. There is said to be peacocks introduced to the Island but we didnt see any.

We enjoyed a lovely tea, then sat in the lounge looking at the many photos and books. Lights went out at 10 oclock when the generator was turned off. Guess who wasn't in bed on time. Margaret! There were lots of possums about at night when you visited the outside loo.

Saturday was another lovely day. Some of the group said that they wished for some rough weather because the lovely days were uncharacteristic of Bass Straight. We went touring the North end of the Island. There was much more vegetation with Eucalyptus and thick tea-tree scrub. We visited Ranger Beach, which is beautifully clean, with a rock formation called 5 sisters at one end. The rocks are covered with orange coloured lichens and beautifully wind and sea sculptured.

Lunch was a picnic overlooking the sea. We saw a seal playing in the sea near a rock platform which had once been a seal colony. Rob said the seals were coming back. We also saw a porpoise and mutton bird rookery. The young birds were in their burrows. At another beach we saw native carvings and over a sand hill a midden. There were a lot of lady finger shells on the beach. We went to the top of the biggest Hummock and had lovely views. Telecom had a communication tower and dish there at one stage but it had been abandoned. All the equipment had been taken down, damaged and just left. Its a mess.

Back at the airstrip while waiting for the homeward flight, Margaret saw a flame scarlet robin rarely seen on the island. We all agreed we had a lovely 2 days and seen most of an Idealic Island.

By Enid Hewitt

Chapter Ten

EAGLE SPIRIT

I had a phone call from one of my sisters that my mother's bowel cancer had come back. She had to go in for another operation. This same sister arranged to be there for the first two weeks to look after my mother, and I agreed to be there for the next two weeks. One of my brothers had given our mother a lot of care before that and in the run-up to the operation. While my mother was under the knife, the surgeon also discovered ovarian cancer and removed as much of that as he could.

A living nightmare then followed as I flew back and forth as often as I could to see my mother, who was slowly dying but not without a great fight. I didn't want my business to fold and would often take work with me.

It was great spending time with my mother, and we made up for lost time after all the years in the UK. In her later years, she had become withdrawn, and our contact had become more and more sporadic. I had always gotten on with my mother, and we had a deep bond. Strangely, in her sickness, mum got her old self back.

I went back every few months. I had tried to get somebody in to look after her, but she wouldn't hear of it. I did manage to get a driver to take her out once a week so that she wasn't stuck at home all of the time and she could also go out with my other sister. My brother had a ute which would only take one passenger, and he took her to the hospital and would take her out for a coffee and on drives into the country, which we were all very grateful to him for.

The first time I went back, the garden had fallen behind, which had been one of my mother's passions. I set about bringing it back to a good condition. "Don't you ever stop," my mother said.

On one trip, we decided to take a break on the East Coast. We met my aunt at a cafe in a colonial town called Evandale and afterwards set off. I had a choice of driving along the highway or going a back route along a dirt road. I followed my feeling and went the slower route. As we rounded a bend, there in front of us were a few Eucalyptus trees on either side of the road. On the road, a great Eagle hovered over the night's roadkill, spreading its wings to appear even larger.

I brought the car to a stop and marvelled at the eagle. I thought the eagle was a sign. In many cultures, the eagle is considered to be the animal of spirit. It is the king of the skies. After a moment, the eagle flew off, and we had the incredible sight of its broad, beating wings. Mum thought I overreacted! The next time I visited, we were in our hometown and just about to go into a museum restaurant, and my mother pointed skyward "Look, an eagle," she said. I gazed upwards, and high in the distance; I saw it circling. I think my mother got that it was a sign and that she would be well looked after when the time came.

Smashing Plates

At another visit to my mother, a relative called in and stayed for tea. In the middle of the conversation, she said, "Smash the plates, and you don't need to wash the dishes," and carried on with her conversation! I was a bit puzzled by this but felt the comment was aimed at me. I was certainly doing all that I could for my mother.

Back in the UK, I had to do a service at Hampton Hill just before Christmas. I came to a lady, and spirit soon identified themselves to her. I was fascinated; a lady came through who was larger than life; she had a strong personality and described herself as theatrical. The woman accepted her immediately; she wore an unusual headdress, and this further confirmed who she was. Spirit changed tack, and I said, "Well, you either have the memory of eating in a Greek restaurant and smashing the plates, or you have a memory of smashing plates!" "All my secrets are coming out here," she replied.

Then, a man came through, identifying himself by saying that he worked at a fair, and again, she accepted him immediately. I saw a saucer with a rose on it, which I incorrectly interpreted and asked, “You know the name Rose?" "No," she said. I went back to spirit, realising I had made the classic mistake and not said what I had seen.

"You can understand one saucer; there is no cup, just a saucer, and there is a rose on it."

"Yes," she said. I then realised that the fairground man had smashed the crockery, and a saucer was all that was left, which was his own unique way of saying that he loved her from the spirit side of life. I could feel that love, and she understood his great affection as well. It turned out that the woman was going to hospital for tests, and the spirit world were crowding around her for support. This man adored his wife despite the fact that he had a temper. He may have broken most of the crockery but dearly loved his wife.

On my next trip to Tasmania, my mother and I went to a weekend market in the neighbouring town of Latrobe. As we parked our car and crossed the road to the market, I felt spirit draw close. I was" frog-marched" by spirit through the market to a specific stall. I found I was looking at crockery. There was a large cake plate with a rose in the middle. On the sign beside it, it said 'Nelson ware $10'. I remembered my guide and realised that spirit were backing me up.

I went over for the last time to be with my mum for her 79th birthday. It was a few days after that that things took a turn for the worse. My mother couldn't stop vomiting, and it turned out she had a collapsed bowel. I was so glad I was there at that time. She had to go in for an operation to sort it out.

As I walked down the hospital's long entrance corridor towards my mother's room, I heard a voice. "A mighty tree has fallen," just as it had for Nelson Mandela.

When I heard that the former activist and South African president had died, that same thought came into my head. Then, when I switched on the TV to watch the funeral, a grandson of his was talking and said those very same words, "A mighty tree has fallen."

Back at the hospital, I repeated that phrase to myself aloud, "A mighty tree has fallen." Then I kept seeing Mrs Durga's face along the corridor and could clearly hear her voice, saying in a matter-of-fact way, "Crossing over is not the big deal that people make out."

"Why is she telling me this?" I thought. I knew before I had finished that thought that my mother was about to pass away. Spirit were preparing me, and those words gave me great strength to get through the ordeal. I told my family members that mum would pass away in a fortnight.

When my mother was discharged to die at home, palliative care, they call it, she was put in the ambulance and driven the 40-minute drive. Her last trip. I didn't get into the ambulance with her as my car was at the hospital, so she went alone. I would probably want to do it on my own, I thought, but after my mother died, she gave me the trip energetically twice, told me off and slapped me, so I realised that I had got it completely wrong and I should have gone with her. It was not a time to be practical, and just because I would have wanted to be alone doesn't mean she had wanted the same thing. I suppose because I have a foot in both spiritual and worldly camps, it is different for me than for most others.

I don't remember how many days my mum took to die at home. She was fully conscious up until the last day and then slipped away. Her children were all with her. I held her hand for her last hours on earth. After her last breath, I closed her eyes and kissed her forehead, then sat with her for a while. For a brief moment, I felt mum blow into my ear.

My brother had asked me to organise the funeral sometime earlier. I was pleased to do this, and it kept me busy. Unbeknownst to him, in a strange way, I felt qualified! I remembered Derek Robinson's funeral and based it on that as much as possible, keeping it a great celebration of her life. I arranged everything and was careful to run it by my siblings before setting things in stone. Everyone agreed on the wording of the eulogy, each making a few changes so that it was unanimous. Afterwards, I realised that I had missed out on mentioning my mother's love of bushwalking, which had been a big part of her life.

Before all the relatives arrived for the funeral, I put an invisible wall up around myself to get me through the funeral as well as the wake, which was being organised by a sister. To add to the strange emotions of that time, it was my 50th birthday three days later.

We met a few days after Mum had passed to divide her possessions. I wasn't sure what to choose, what would remind me most of my mother. Being the youngest, I rightly was the fifth and last to choose. I chose an old oil painting of the local area with the mountain in the distance that we grew up in front of Mount Roland. One brother chose a beautiful painting of a pink blossom by a well-known Tasmanian artist. The other brother chose sets of knives for his daughters, which were wedding presents to my Mum and Dad. My eldest sister chose our grandmother's treasured engagement ring and my other sister went for a camphor wood chest, which had been a wedding gift to my mother.

Funnily enough, the picture I chose, as nice as it is, doesn't remind me of mum; it just reminds me of a very sad time. Going through Mum's photos, I found an old letter she had written. When her father died, she inherited some money and, apart from loaning money to her children, she went on many trips. The letter I found was a description of one of her holidays to a remote Island off Tasmania, 3 Hummock Island. Whenever I read this, I hear my mother's voice and these two pages help to keep our bonds strong.

In my mother's hall, for a number of years, she had a photo in a frame of me smiling on a beach on Flinders Island. This is where we were first brought up. Above and below the picture, my mother had put photos of the mountains of Flinders Island. My sister and I had revisited the island years later on one of my trips back home. A local remembered our family and gave us a box of mutton birds to give to our father. We divided them into two and gave half to Mum and half to Dad.

After my mother had died, I was the only one in the house. It seemed strange, staying there alone. After splitting some of her material goods, with the remainder to be auctioned off, I walked down the hall and spotted the picture of me on Flinders Island. I took it off the wall and gazed at it. Well, I have enough pictures of myself, I thought, but it meant something to my mother. I had, in fact, asked her sometime before why she had the picture in the hall. "Because I like it." she had answered with a twinkle in her eye. Because she liked it, I'll take it, I decided, and took it back to my room, 'the boy's room' as Mum used to call it.

As I put it with the Mersey picture, the one with the mountain in the background, the frame became loose, and the glass shifted. I gasped. There behind the backing was another picture, an old Pears print. I recognised it immediately, as it had been hung at my grandparent's house throughout my childhood. It was my grandfather's favourite picture of four tethered horses. Strangely enough, I had just bought a picture of an untethered horse as a present to myself for my 50th, a fifth horse!

It was a great comfort to me to find this picture. Clearly, my mother wanted me to have it. She must have hidden it all those years ago when her father had died, and she, in turn, got an inheritance. It made me feel special during this awful time and made me feel connected to my mother. The print was of no particular value, but it was incredibly precious to me. When my mother died, I thought that if I had all the money and material treasure in the world, it wouldn't amount to more than one moment more with my mother. I would trade it all in the blink of an eye.

A few weeks before I left for Australia for my mother's 79th birthday, I was near Winchester for work. I was suddenly gripped by a compulsion to treat myself for a change and to buy something for my upcoming 50th. I stopped in Alresford and went into a shop. I was a bit robot-like, and I was being guided by spirit, as with the rose plate. Either that or I just don't like shopping and wanted to get it over and done with as quickly as possible! I was born in the Chinese year of the horse, and there in the shop was a print from a run of 100 by a well-known animal artist. It was of a white horse, unfettered, running free. To me, it represented freedom. I made up my mind in an instant and made the purchase. My birthday present to myself.

For my birthday, just three days after my mother's funeral, my best friend from school and his family made a great effort to cheer me up and took me out for a meal. I was so grateful for their kindness at a horrible time.

After I returned to the UK, I felt my mother around me a lot. Twice, I got out of bed, and there was a palpable energy of her saying, "If my treatment was different, I would still be alive today." I realise now she was probably trying to extend the lives of others in the same fate. The cause of death on her death certificate was different to what she died of, but at the time, I was full of grief and just thought, "What is the point, my mother is gone, and it won't bring her back." She could have lived a lot longer.

When my mother went over to the other side, she had a look into it. I don't doubt for a moment that she was 100 per cent correct.

Chapter Eleven

GUIDANCE FROM ABOVE

At first, I didn't want to call a medium for a reading as I felt that if the medium didn't bring my mother through properly, it would be an insult to her. Also, why couldn't my mum come through directly to me? (Which she did anyway.) I didn't want to reduce my mother to a message!

Mum did communicate to me with ideas. I was sitting in the lounge when suddenly I had a strong memory of radiator covers! A week later, I was walking into a garden centre, and there, by the entrance, was a big advert for bespoke radiator covers. I knew it was my mother arranging it, so I promptly put smart covers over my ugly radiators. Soon after, I was sat in the same place, and I had the idea to put a door on the empty doorway between my two front rooms. I knew it was my mother, so I set about fitting a door. As it turned out, these were both great improvements. My mother was being very practical and modifying my house! I had lived in this house for seven years and never had these ideas.

I had thought for a while that I needed to take the office out of my home. It had been in the front room, and although I had rented offices in the past, I thought it was time to get my house back, as I was becoming busier and busier. I did eventually have a phone reading. Mum came through and said that I was not to give up looking for an office. I had looked but had yet to come up with anything suitable. For that to be mentioned, I knew immediately that the ideal office was out there right now.

That weekend, I drove around Kingston, crossed the river, and jotted down telephone numbers from billboards before asking my office admin to search for a place based on these contacts. Straight away, she found the perfect office! I knew it was my mother's influence, just as I knew at the time that I had to act quickly. The new office was a studio with a small courtyard. It could not have been more ideal and very well priced, so I snapped the rental up safe in the knowledge that Mum had tipped me off at just the right moment.

A few months later, still deeply in grief, as I was walking home, I spotted a poster pinned to a telegraph pole. Thinking it was a plea for a lost cat, I went up to read it: a psychic evening at the Willoughby, a local pub a few streets away. "Oh good!" I thought, not being a church, nobody would know me! I didn't want a reading, but I was feeling so bad still after Mum passed; I just wanted some healing.

Portobello Road

I eventually phoned a friend who was a respected medium. She brought through my mother and gave me some strong evidence. In the reading, she told me that my mother said I should go to Portobello Road. At that time, I was franticly busy at work, and as I had better things to do, I thought I would give it a miss. I also thought that if it were from my mother, she would have something more important to say than to visit Portobello Road!

Portobello Road is a prime tourist destination on market day, with antique stalls and shops. The bottom end is more for selling street food, and beyond that, there are fruit and vegetable stalls that cater for the locals. My school friend who had just been over from Australia had just visited the market, and I had been myself many years ago. Some months later, I called my medium friend again to get another reading. She again gave me a lot of detail and dropped into the conversation about going to Portobello Road.

As this was such a seemingly random comment that had been mentioned twice, I realised that it must be important and that I had to take heed. I immediately resolved to go on the next market day.

I thought I might see an identical object that had belonged to mother. I searched Portobello Road on the internet, checked market day and the best time to go and set off. I remembered that the medium had also mentioned on both occasions, cobbled streets. I approached the market and drove over to the Notting Hill Gate end. I glanced at the road surface. It was tarmac. There were throngs of tourists, and as I drove around searching for a car park, I soon realised the chances of finding a free space were extremely slim. I had landscaped and maintained several gardens a few streets away on the other side of Ladbroke Grove, so I headed that way, knowing all the parking meters in that area. I was in luck; I found a space, parked up and walked back past Starbucks and Cafe Nero, past the reggae and Caribbean stalls at Ladbroke Grove and over to Westbourne Park, past the hardware store I often used for work and took a right into Portobello Road.

I thought I would be faced with an object and entered the market with a great air of expectation. On past the fruit and veg stalls I went, noting that the road was still tarmac, through the street food stalls, and then on up the hill. The throngs of tourists got thicker the higher up the hill I went, and the road was still very much tarmac. The food stalls made way to ones selling antiques of every kind imaginable. Further up the hill, I climbed. Suddenly, I became aware that the crowd ahead had hushed. People had fallen silent and were looking around, bewildered. I hurried forward, knowing it had something to do with my mother!

There in the middle of the crowd, darting in and out in broad daylight, was a fox: "My mother", I thought again. It's not that I thought my mother had turned into a fox, you understand, but that she had sent it as a guide! I knew that I had to follow the fox. Its tail was damaged. How the poor thing had come to lose half its brush, I didn't know. Everybody was bemused, smiling and marvelling at a fox in a crowd in the middle of London. I followed it. It darted down a cobbled street, turned around and scurried off. It has led me here, I thought. I clocked the spot and continued to walk up the hill in case it became cobbled at the other end. Before too long, I reached the Notting Hill Gate end with no cobble in sight! I returned to the little mews road and surveyed the sight in front of me, arms crossed. The first stall on the corner sold bric-a-brac with some nice old watering cans and wooden handled trowels. "Nice," I thought, but it wasn't for me. I turned to the other side of the mews, a rock and crystal stall. "No, not for me either."

I turned to the final stand. There were dozens and dozens of Tupperware tubs filled with antique prints. "This is it," I thought. I walked along the row with my hand outstretched, 'scanning' the tubs before stopping at the third tub along and lifting the first print up. Nothing. I pulled up the second print. Nothing. I pulled up the third print. Again nothing. I moved on to the fourth print and pulled it up. I stared hard. It was an antique etching, and below it read 'Red-necked wallaby, Tasmanian variety'. I was staring at a pair of wallabies.

I didn't know whether to laugh or cry. It had meant so much to me that my mother had wanted me to have the picture behind the picture at her home. Obviously, this was another picture she wanted me to see. There were a few more coloured etchings of Tasmanian animals. I should have bought the lot! I spoke to the owner, and he said he also had a map. He pulled out a 100-plus-year-old Tasmanian map. It had been sliced up into several counties of England. I bought both and left, feeling delighted.

After this, the fish tank episode, and Derek saying that it was "very multidimensional over there," I thought I had an understanding of spirit coincidences. I had been told by spiritualists many times that there was no time in spirit. I believe that when you die, you can go backwards or forwards in time and quite literally anywhere apart from what is beyond the frequency of your soul.

So perhaps when my grandmother died, she had a look at my life. She looked into my past and saw how I had been hard on myself over making a pass to the Danish girl. And so, when I was doing symbols, she put the image of the Eiffel Tower into my mind. She knew that it would be very difficult for me when my mother passed away, and all those years ago, she put the symbol of the fish tank in my mind, then influenced me with the eulogy and influenced another of her daughters to send me the notes. How else would I get such a strange symbol all those years later?

Later that same day, I was in a lighting shop looking to change the bathroom light when I saw some hall lanterns. There was a very nice one, very small, that would go perfectly at the top of my stairs. I looked at the price tag and thought perhaps I wouldn't. A breeze blew into my ear. I looked around to see if anyone had just come into the shop to create the breeze by opening the door. There was no one there. I remember when my mother blew into my ear just after she died. I'll buy the light I resolved and treat myself if my mum wants me to have it.

That night, I was working at a spiritual church for their Saturday night clairvoyance evening, and I wondered what would come through after this turn of events. I had taken my suit with me, so I didn't have to go back and forth across London. I spent some time at a Thai restaurant in Golders Green before heading off for the 7.30 start. It was an unusual evening for me as I didn't feel there was much energy. A man came through and described himself, speaking with a powerful and commanding voice.

"You wouldn't dare not do as he said," I suggested.

"Yes," the recipient said, knowing who he was.

"There is someone around you that you need to have words with."

"Yes," she agreed.

"He will be with you to help." The booming voice held great power. Then, my mind went to Martin Luther King. "He was an admirer of Martin Luther King?" I asked.

"Oh yes."

"They have met," I told the lady.

The next day, I heard a recording of his voice on a TV advert. Was that just a coincidence, or was it spirit backing me up?

The Joseph Coat

I awoke to a dream. "So where is your Joseph coat?" I heard. It was my mother. A week later, I visited a furniture store, looking to pick something up in the January sales. As I walked in, there in the foyer was a rolled-up rug with a tag on it declaring "Joseph rug." It was a burnt orange rug, striped with many colours. Of course, I had to buy it after the dream, and I had just the place for it! I then read the story of Joseph. I understood the archetype.

Sometimes, when I had a reading, the medium would say that my mother could see what I was up to now that she was on the other side. So much more than from Australia when she was alive! She was happy about that.

Statue at the End of the Bed

I got ready to go to bed, turned out the light and climbed under the duvet. In the gloom, I saw a figure a few feet away. "Mum," I thought and peered forward. There in front of me was a statue of Mother Mary! My first thought was that my mother was playing a joke on me, that she had gone into my mind and latched on to when I had seen Jesus' eyes in China and knew that I had wished to see Mary! Exhausted after a long day, I dropped back into the pillow and fell asleep.

Paula's Reading

The evening came for the psychic pub night at the Willoughby. I thought it would be nice to do something outside the spiritual churches where nobody would know me. It was a Friday night. After a hard day's work, my energy wasn't that great, to be honest. I didn't want a reading from my mother; I wanted healing as I was still feeling grief-stricken and didn't want to "reduce her to a message," so to speak.

I walked into the pub and was instantly greeted with "Hello Jeff." I looked up and saw a lady. I recognised her face but could not place where I knew her from or, should I say, from which spiritual church I knew her.

"I've come for some healing," I said, whereupon one of the three ladies who were there gave me some healing. Paula asked me to sit myself down, and she would give me a reading. She told me that when I had come in, my mother had come in behind me. Paula gave me a marvellous reading from my mum. It was very meaningful, and I understood it all, except for the very last thing. She didn't "reduce my mother to a reading."

"She gives you a white rosary," Paula told me. I was baffled by that as my mother in life was not a religious person. Certainly, we were not Catholics and were from Methodist origins. I wondered if my mother had met the nun! Well, I need not have worried as I had my answer just a few days later. On the Sunday I was booked to take a Sunday service at Clapham Common. I arrived early, and after going into the quiet room, which doubled as a kitchen, I immediately saw a cardboard box on top of the cupboard with a picture of a statue of Mary. I reached up and took it down for a closer look. It was a biscuit box of Fatima from Portugal. I read the English script about how the three peasant children had received visitations from the Holy Mother, standing in a tree and holding a white rosary! I immediately remembered what Paula had said.

Lourdes Postcard

I was still grieving deeply for my mother, and after Paula's reading and seeing the white rosary on the box, I felt it was a sign to go to that place. I wanted to do something physical to get over my mother's passing and help with the loss process. I Googled Fatima and the vision of Mary. Two sites came up, one being Lourdes. I had heard about Lourdes, of course, with its healing waters, and purely because it was easier to get a train with one change in Paris, I organised a trip. I got off the train and crossed the road to the hotel I was staying in, admiring the snow-capped Pyrenees on the distant horizon before making my way to the complex.

It was January, and the place was virtually deserted; the countless souvenir shops, which must have stretched along the road for a mile and a half, were all closed for the winter season, with the exception of a clutch of shops in front of the entrance to the religious complex. It was approaching evening, and I had three days in Lourdes, so I thought I would have a quick look around and then come back the next day for a proper exploration. I went into the large church, where a massive statue of Saint Peter sat in a chair, holding a key, then walked down to the river to see the alcove in the rock face where the village girl Bernadette had experienced her visions of Mary. It had been a long day, so I walked back to the hotel and got a good night's sleep in preparation for my day of exploration.

The next day, as I stood in the forecourt, gazing at the grand church in front of me, my mobile phone rang. I pulled it out of my pocket and looked at the screen. It was an Australian number, my sister Marie, who never ever called me.

"You will never guess where I am," I blurted out.

"Where are you?"

"Lourdes," I answered, "I got the train..." We chatted for a bit.

"Isn't that the place with the healing waters?" Marie asked.

"Yes," I replied, "But I have come here to help me get over mum's death."

We spoke for a little while longer, and then after we had said our goodbyes, I walked back up the slope to the souvenir shops. Browsing through the postcards, one stood out. It was a photograph of the mosaic above the high altar of the church. It read "Marie and Jesus", and in the middle was a picture of an angel that looked just like Marie's niece on her husband's side, Jessica. I bought the postcard and sent it to her. She called me a few weeks later, 'tickled pink,' to receive the 'personalised card'. I thought my mother was playing a joke on us!

Back in Lourdes, I went to the information desk and enquired about the healing waters.

"Just turn up between these times," the lady said, assuring me that I didn't need to take anything when I asked about a towel. She also directed me to an underground church, which I made my first port of call. It was built of concrete and was the size of a football pitch, with large banners displaying a picture of a different saint on each banner hung around the walls. I made my way slowly around the empty chapel, looking up at each saint before reading about them on a small plaque located beneath each banner. Back upstairs in the open air, I felt my mother was around me again and heard her say, "Well, what about me?" I had a good cry, and it was what I needed and felt a release.

On the second day, I caught the bus to the distant Pyrenees. After the bus had been travelling for a while, I looked back towards where we had come from. It was a picturesque valley scene, with Lourdes nestled in the middle. I got my phone out and took a picture.

On the screen, there was a glow right over Lourdes! "The church would pay a lot of money for that photo," I thought. Then I pressed the delete button by accident!

As the bus carried on and began climbing into the mountains, I was reminded of a service I had done a couple of weeks earlier. A man had come through and asked, "Do you remember the time we drove up the mountain, around all of those hairpin bends, eventually getting to the top and sitting in the car, admiring the view? And what a view, it was worth it."

Sitting on the bus, I realised we were going through a series of hairpin bends. I could feel the movement in my body, the same as in the reading I had just given a fortnight before. "Well, the view will be worth it at the top," I thought!

On the final day of my trip, I decided to take the healing waters, when in Rome! I didn't have a clue what to expect. I arrived early and waited on the trestle benches outside a large metal door. There were two doors set apart, one for men and another for women. Not knowing what was behind the doors or why the men and women were kept separate, my mind went to the Second World War! Not a good feeling and the opposite of the one I was supposed to feel.

Gradually, more people arrived and sat by me. I could imagine that at the height of the season, one could wait for hours and hours for this experience. At last, the half a dozen of us were ushered into a cubicle and told to undress, leaving on our underwear. As I was at the front of the queue, I was the first to go and emerged from behind a second curtain to be faced by a French priest and his two attendants, one on either side of a large marble bath. The priest instructed me to face the wall, then he held up an apron to cover my modesty and told me to take my underwear off and put it in the plastic bag hanging on a hook. Standing completely naked, the priest then wrapped the apron around me and tied it up. Decent again, I faced the bath as the priest uttered some prayers in French.

The two attendants appeared at my side, each taking one of my elbows and leading me into the ankle-deep water, where I was pulled backwards and dunked into the water. They then handed me a jug and invited me to wash myself, just as the vision of Mary had instructed Bernadette to do. I said my own prayer to myself and my spirit guides.

"Have a good pilgrimage." One of the attendees said. The process was reversed before I returned to the changing room, dripping wet in my damp undies.

"Where is the towel?" I asked the attendant.

"Dress wet," he replied, "the water is holy!"

Walking out into the cold January morning, the water evaporated, and I was soon as warm as toast. I felt euphoric.

Like most visitors to Lourdes, I bought bottles to fill and take back to

London. I bought five small bottles and filled them from the designated taps.

About a month after coming back, I was asked to take a Sunday service at Hackbridge, the sister church to Wimbledon. I was asked if I wanted to take part in a fundraiser. This was for a woman whose dying wish was to go to Lourdes. "I've just been," I said. I gave the lady some travel tips and agreed to join in with the fundraising.

A few weeks after that, I awoke to a dream from my mother. "I did a Lazarus," she said. "I was put in a box, and I climbed out!"

The Snake & Truganini

I needed more time after Lourdes as I still had a lot of grieving to do. I wanted to do something practical again, so I set off to Devon for a four-day break to switch off from work and to try and put myself back together. I got the evening train from Paddington and booked the Travelodge opposite Exeter station. Apart from that night, I hadn't booked anywhere as I thought I would "follow my nose" and most likely stay by the coast.

Realising I was so close to Exeter cathedral, I thought it would be foolish not to visit it; so bright and early the next morning, I set off for the city centre, stopping to ask for directions. As instructed, I walked up a narrow lane and turned right at the top into a residential street. The lady had said to go straight over the roundabout, which I did. Then, suddenly, I felt snakes wrapping themselves around my legs. Ugh! I swept the thought aside with my mind, but back they came, even stronger. It was an extraordinary sensation, but I kept walking before sending a thought up to God, "What are you telling me? I'm doomed?" "Well, if I am doomed, what can I do? I thought and continued on my way. The snakes faded away.

I continued to follow the directions and, before long, was passing a row of shops. As you can imagine, I was unsettled by my experience. I had welcomed all of my previous experiences with open arms, feeling privileged to have phenomena happen. This one, however, I found unnerving. I started to window shop and then stopped in my tracks. A window display was of small bird cages but with no birds in them. This was a piece of evidence I had given a lady at a service the week before. She had agreed that she had a cage but with no birds in it. "Well, that's a comfort," I thought, "free as a bird is way better than being strangled by a snake!" I walked on and spent the next hour or so caught up in the beauty of the cathedral, followed by some retail therapy. The snake experience faded away, and I returned to my usual self.

As I made my way back to the station, from where I had decided to head for Exmouth, I noticed a lot of people coming in and out of a museum. "That looks popular," I thought and ventured inside. It was a fascinating place, and I made my way around it, delighting in collections garnered from Victorian explorers and rooms crammed with stuffed animals. Other rooms featured collections from indigenous people. I admired an Eskimo waterproof jacket, which must have been 200 years old. I left the room with the Eskimo collection and turned into another when I was stopped in my tracks, my mouth agape. There in front of me was a stuffed mongoose with a snake wrapped around it, with its head looking back at the mongoose. My morning's experience came rushing back to me.

Out of the corner of my eye, I saw, located in the same cabinet, a picture. It was of Truganini, one of Tasmania's last full-blood aborigines who was known for a long time in her country as the last of her race. There she was, in the cabinet looking out at me. I burst into tears. I read the caption beneath the picture. Her necklace and bracelet had been housed at the museum until they were returned to the Tasmanian people in the 1970s. This solved the riddle of this morning's snake!

Later that day, I arrived in Exmouth. The place was uncannily like the north-west coast of Tasmania, and I felt my mother around me. In fact, while in Exmouth, I felt her presence with me constantly. As I looked over the water to the land on the other side of the estuary, it reminded me of the view from the bluff in Devonport over to the national park in the distance, with dotted farmland in the foreground.

As I made my way to the Jurassic Coast, walking beside the cliff face, I was reminded of the walk up Don Heads in Tasmania. As I got to the top and looked along the coastline, I brought back vivid memories of the north-west coast of Tasmania, looking west. The estuary was full of yachts and was very reminiscent of the Tamar Valley in Tasmania. Earlier, I had passed a Ferris wheel. This had been a symbol that I had received when doing a reading for someone just a week or so before. The message I had given to that person was that everything had gone full circle. I could fully agree with that for myself; I thought as I readied myself for the next chapter in my life.

I felt that I was being bombarded by spirit, and starting to see signs in everything after my mother's passing. I was close to a form of madness. I took a step back and 'pressed the reset button.' I was thankful for the gardening to keep myself grounded and sane. It was ironic too that through the earth's energies, I was allowed to look into the spiritual dimension in such a deep fashion. A delicate balance was maintained and no hole was burnt in my energy as I continued my work.

Chapter Twelve

LIFE IS LIKE A SERIES OF CHAPTERS

Years earlier, I had a gardening client in Mayfair who said, "Life is like a series of chapters." At the time, I remember thinking what a load of corny rubbish, but as I grew older, I realised how right she was!

A Windsor Ghost

I was due to work at Windsor Church again. After the episode, when I arrived very late, I made a point of getting there early, even having time for some Christmas shopping and enjoying lunch in one of the town's many cafes and eateries. The church itself was very well laid out, with lovely artwork on the walls. In the sanctuary, there were always candles alight and all manner of fake flower decorations! On this occasion, there was a delightful bouquet of peace lilies in the fireplace. This was all above a shop in what used to be a flat, until it was bequeathed to the church by its former owner.

With time still on my hands, I wandered into the parish church over the road, walking around its quiet interior before lighting two candles in memory. There were a few other people there, dotted around in the pews, and I joined them and sat a while in silence. Out of nowhere, a spirit person walked towards me. He was wearing 17th-century clothes, had a pointy face, was middle-aged and wore a large round collar. As he walked in my direction, he faded away. Wow, had I just seen a ghost? He looked like Charles I or Shakespeare!

I got up from my pew and walked past some tables strewn with pamphlets. The first one that caught my eye was all about the work that particular church was doing in Africa. The next one featured an etching of a man with a square collar, a man that looked remarkably similar to the one I had just seen, though the collar was different. It was advertising a play, The Merry Wives of Windsor, and the etching was of William Shakespeare. Had I just seen the ghost of William Shakespeare? Two mediums later said that I had him around me. I wasn't very good with words, so I wasn't sure what he would want with me, or had I simply seen him as his imprint was there? Never the less I welcomed the sighting.

A Run of Bagpipes

My Kent friend Stephen had lent me a handwritten book that his aunt had written as an autobiography detailing her spiritual life. They knew it would be of interest to me. Meanwhile, my childhood friend Chris and his partner came over to the UK for a holiday. Chris was my best friend from my school days, and we met up for dinner and went to the Chinese two doors down from where I lived, before giving them a tour of my little house. The very next day, I was driving around for work, and through the open window of my van, I could just hear, very faintly, the sound of bagpipes. I listened hard, straining; yes, I could definitely hear it oh so faintly. I thought that it was my spiritual ear, and I knew that my friend was somewhere listening to bagpipe music at that very moment. Or perhaps it was Clairbagpipe! The battery on my mobile was flat, so it wasn't until the evening that I was able to send a text.

"Great day. Did you hear any Scottish bagpipes?"

He replied, "Well, you must be psychic. I was at the British Museum and heard someone playing bagpipes!"

I replied that it was 'my spiritual ear', showing off to him.

"How weird," was my friend's bemused reply.

I thought that was the end of the story, but it was not to be the case. A few weeks later, Chris and his partner were to be back in London after their tour of Britain, and I thought it would be nice to go to a show of some kind. Seeing that the Proms were on, I snapped up tickets, thinking that Chris would appreciate being in the Albert Hall, especially for such a British occasion. I wasn't wrong, and we all had a marvellous evening. The concert finished, and we made our way out with the throng. It had been a hot summer's day, and the evening was welcomingly cool. As we walked back towards the van, again, I heard the faint bagpipe music.

"Chris," I exclaimed, pulling at his sleeve, "the bagpipes."

He didn't say anything. We walked on and saw the piper packing up and getting on his bike. He rode down Exhibition Road to catch the passing crowd, where he set up pitch again. The bagpipe music droned out as we neared.

The next day, I carried on reading Stephen's great aunt's book. I turned the page, and there she was, as a girl out with her uncle rowing a boat across a loch.

"What lovely bagpipe music," she said.

"What bagpipes?" asked her uncle.

It turned out that she too, had heard them spiritually. Her uncle told her that it is said that they signal a death in the McDonald clan. Sure enough, the book recounted that a few days after that boat trip on the loch, her poorly mother took a turn for the worse and passed away.

I wondered why I had heard the bagpipes, then realised that it was simply that I had spent the evening before with Chris and his partner, showing them my house and going to a restaurant. As I was so familiar with his energy, I simply connected to what was going on in his energy at the time. As the pipes are so shrill and piercing, it is distinctive on one's energy.

Nobody was about to die. Meeting Chris and his friend on the last night of their trip, I thought it was a great tease to read him the chapter from my friend's book!

Sometime after, while visiting Tasmania, it was my last day, and Chris had kindly offered to drop me off at the airport. We had some time before I was due to board, so we stopped along the way for a coffee. This was a very small town surrounded by farmland, and as we drank our coffee, someone in the distance started to play the bagpipes! Chris looked at me nervously. We agreed it was weird after those other experiences in London! I was convinced my mother was playing a joke on him, as it was the last place one would expect to hear bagpipes!

A Homage

As I had heard Mrs Durga's voice when my mother died, I thought it was important to pay homage to her and visit India. I was due for a holiday, so I booked a flight. I felt it might be wise to go with a group, so I headed to my local travel agent and booked myself a guided eleven-day tour. With my mother's inheritance, I had decided to do one 'spend' on a special trip for myself.

I met the group in Delhi, where the plane had landed, just as the trip was starting. I fell on my feet and was with a terrific group made up of both singles and couples. Going on your own is always a risk, especially in somewhere as hectic as India. Soon after arriving, I succumbed to 'Delhi belly' but quickly shook it off, and we joked later that it was just 'belly!' The food was so good.

I can't say that I felt Mrs Durga around me at all in Jaipur, but that was fine; I certainly wasn't going to call on anyone in that way. One morning, I came downstairs in the hotel in Jaipur in preparation of setting off for the day. I went up to talk to a girl in the group, and each time I went to speak, I choked on my words. My mouth would open, but nothing would come out. After several times of trying but failing, I paused and managed to tell her, "I just can't speak!"

Afterwards, I realised somebody in the spirit world had drawn close and given me that they had a speech impediment from a stroke. The next day, I went up to this girl when she was alone and said, "I hope you don't mind me saying, but I wondered if you knew anybody upstairs who had a stroke." I pointed skywards as I said that, hoping she knew what I was getting at!

"I'm a physiotherapist and sometimes work with people who have had strokes," she said. I didn't want to push it any further as I felt uncomfortable reading for someone who hadn't asked for it.

We had great adventures being driven through the chaotic traffic and experiencing all the awe-inspiring sights, sounds and smells. At the end of the day, one was dazed as the senses had been constantly bombarded.

The main leg of the trip finished at the Taj Mahal, where a splinter group, myself included, would then go off to Orcha and onto Varanasi on the mighty Ganges. We had barely arrived at the bustle of life when a dead body was carried past us on a bamboo stretcher! A few hours later, we saw a pyre being lit in the distance. We thought we might have seen earlier who was on that. Varanasi was even more hectic than Jaipur had been.

At Orcha, there was a stencil on the wall for decoration; it was of three bird cages with their doors open and distant birds in flight. It immediately reminded me of the shop display in the Exeter jewellers and, with it, coming through as a piece of evidence at a service. I thought, do I take that as a sign? I certainly had the first time. At Orcha, I had opted for an early morning safari trip at the Panna Wildlife Reserve. I had convinced myself that I wouldn't see a thing, and then saw three majestic tigers. What sleek, regal beasts they were. I remembered years earlier in my evening class, sitting in meditation, and out of nowhere, a tiger's energy walked right beside me. Here I was all those years later, right beside a tiger as one glided by the jeep.

I also had a 'run' of pictures of tigers at several services I held. I would say to the recipients that they had a picture of a tiger, and they would say "yes" every time! My father had a large oil painting of a tiger, which he had since before I was born.

Later in the trip, I stayed in Varanasi, beside the Ganges. Here, the hotel was changed as the one we were supposed to be in was fully booked. I was surprised to see the same stencil on the wall again. "Ok, I get it," I thought up to spirit. "Stay free, and don't allow yourself to be put in a cage, even one of your own making."

On the plane back from India, I settled down to watch a film that a group member had recommended. About 15 minutes in, there was a scene about a bird of freedom woven into a carpet. I remembered the empty bird cages. Some people only find their freedom after passing. We need to navigate through life and retain that sense of freedom as best we can.

More Services

I arrived at a church for a service and sat in their quiet room where the medium would open up. I came out from the waiting room through to the door directly connected to the platform. I remembered years before seeing 'demonstrations' as they call them, evenings of clairvoyance, where the medium would appear on the platform from a side door, just like an actor about to perform. The congregation would hush, and there would be an air of expectation in the room. The big difference is that an actor learns his lines in advance, whereas a medium has no script. What he does have is faith and a toolbox of techniques to link to the spirit world. With practice, the medium builds up familiarity and can very quickly launch into his or her work.

Sometimes, when working, spirit will start to give you a sentence, and you have no idea what you are about to say. It is that same feeling as being blindfolded and being asked to walk forward. It is a great test of faith. It is only after voicing the first part of the sentence that spirit then give you the second part. Often, spirit will give you very bizarre information, and you ask yourself, do I really have to say that? Once, they showed me a monkey. "Yes, he had a pet monkey," the response came back. You learn to say what spirit gives you.

I sat down as the chairperson opened the meeting and introduced me. I gave an opening prayer, and we all sang along to a hymn. I was asked to 'demonstrate my gifts of the spirit' as they would say.

I gave out the name Charles, gypsy connections and a man with a King Charles spaniel. Who can understand these three points? I asked, having no idea myself who the information was for. There was silence. I went on, Irish connections and the recipient would understand a memory of a horseshoe hanging on a wall. A lady shyly acknowledged. Various information then flowed, and about four people were mentioned to this lady. A woman in the spirit world showed me her feet: before she died, she had suffered from swollen feet. Spirit gave me this, along with the feelings that the woman had experienced.

I must have served this church once a month as they would often text and see if I was free at short notice. It was set in an old school, in the library that was rented out. Methodists in the morning and spiritualists in the evening, which clashed with the Pentecostals who had band practice next door! Every Sunday, the table would be put into position, the chairs set out, and the hymn books placed on each seat. The table was covered with a lace tablecloth and upon it a large brass cross, a healing book, the usual jug of water and a vase of fresh flowers, always a bunch of either carnations or chrysanthemums.

A perk for the medium was that he or she would be given the bunch of flowers to take home. These carnations would keep for about a month in my house, and I would marvel at how long they would last. This particular evening, I went to six people, which was good going for me as I usually stayed too long with one person. The SNU's (Spiritualist National Union) recommendation was to stay seven minutes with every recipient. I would stay for as long as I felt the spirit wanted me to stay.

After Christmas, I did a service at the Clapham Spiritualist Church (or the 'a list church' as the sign said, due to someone having scratched off some letters!) On the day before, I had drunk too many wines. I awoke in the morning not feeling very bright.

I readied myself for the day and went outside to drive to a cafeteria for breakfast. I crossed the road towards my van. The lamp post in the centre of the road had a light on each side to light the street. Suddenly, this changed, and the arms for the light extended, and suddenly, it was a cross with Jesus nailed to it. The next instant, it was gone, like the vision of Mary. I hadn't been feeling the least bit spiritual at the time! The vision was accompanied by a pious feeling.

That evening at the church, a woman came through. She was an aunt to the recipient. A spinster aunt, two sisters, one was a nun. I realised in a moment that she had given me the morning vision. I explained to the congregation what had happened that morning, that I had thought I was having a spiritual experience when it turned out to be this lady's aunt! Everybody laughed! Never before had I met someone so devout. She lived and breathed for the Lord. I conveyed all of this to the recipient, and she agreed. A few weeks earlier, I had felt a nail driven through my hand. Now I knew what it was all about. The Nun was impressing things upon me.

After my mother died, I wondered if she knew all about my mediumship and how it had taken up so much of my life. I wondered if she knew about my spiritual drive, which I had kept to myself. Maybe she mentioned the white rosary to prove that she did know? Maybe she mentioned the white rosary as she knew my wish to meet the Holy Mother or the sacred feminine after my trip to Pakistan and China all those years ago? Was she pointing out her own holy aspects now that she was in the spirit world? I remembered Mum's piece of driftwood, which she called 'mother and child.' The mother was veiled and was very much like Mary. After my mother died, I realised everybody has their own Mary and have spent time with Mary. She is your own mother.

I hadn't been in touch with the yoga group for a few years. Before Christmas, I received an invitation to their harvest festival, a celebration of what they had achieved as a group. When I was in my late forties, I realised that I was not where I wanted to be in life regarding financial security and that my business was not where I wanted it to be. I resolved to knuckle down and build the business up. My social life suffered as a result, and I neglected my friends. I continued to work as a medium, accepting any bookings that came along, but as I was no longer in a development group, the social aspect of that side of things subsided as well. Then, when my mother became ill, my frequent trips to Tasmania meant my English life became all work and no play! I wouldn't have changed any of it, though, as I had to visit my mother at every opportunity I could.

So when the invitation came through to see the yogis, I jumped at the chance. As the time approached, it was mentioned that part of the afternoon would be a discussion on what they were doing as a group and an opportunity for people to join the group. I remained silent as they talked, as I didn't want to express an interest, as it was a commitment that I could not give.

As I sat there, suddenly, my mouth opened, and words came out: "So there are no shortcuts then?"

"Absolutely not," the leader replied, "not one iota."

I tried to look normal despite being so surprised that I had spoken. That was trance, I thought; I had blurted the words out involuntarily.

I left wondering if I was taking a spiritual shortcut in my life, which I knew would never work. No stone can be left unturned in one's spiritual unfoldment. The day before I was due to go to Lourdes, I had gone to the printers to get some plans scanned and emailed on a pdf file. Andy helped me out and handed the screen over to me so I could write my personal message before the plans were sent. I noticed the file heading, "Shortcuts Jeff."

"Why is that written there," I asked.

"I don't know," Andy had replied.

A Skin Graft & a Good Demonstration at Kingston

I felt like a complete fool at Morden church when I had brought through to an elderly man:

"Have you burnt yourself standing too close to a radiator?"

"I have," he answered honestly.

Spirit immediately said that he had a skin graft from an unmentionable area.

"Yes," he agreed.

"Well, you won't be doing that again in a hurry," I said.

"That's for sure," the old man answered.

Occasionally, I would do two demonstrations on a Sunday. On this occasion, I was doing my first in Wimbledon for their 11am service, followed by a 6.30 at Kingston. The morning dem went ok, and I was pleased to give Kelly, a blind girl, a reading. Spirit spoke about sand between her toes. She said she had been talking about that recently as it was a strange sensation to a blind person to have the ground beneath your feet move for the first time on the beach!

With another person, spirit spoke about dandelions and the need to get them out at the root. I took this as a message for myself with somebody at work who I realised was a bad egg, not a good worker at all and thought spirit were confirming that they should be ousted as they were not doing my company any favours. Sure enough, two more email complaints soon followed, and the member of staff was dismissed.

In the evening, I was at Kingston. Spirit came in with a bang, and I knew immediately who I was with.

"You knew somebody who worked at a fun fair?"

"Yes," a lady said.

They gave it to me so clearly that it was like I was there. Spirit went on to give this lady a wealth of facts and information. Later, a man came through for her and said, "Thank you for looking after me." She burst into tears. I think she needed to hear that.

Her mother came through, and then her grandmother, who was a larger-than-life character. She was a Romany gypsy and very proud of it. "I used to read the tea leaves," she said. Spirit showed me a birdcage with no bird in it!

"Yes, I know that," she said, it is in my home. Going back to the funfair, I said that she had been on a Ferris wheel. "Yes," she said.

Somebody in the spirit world kept saying "Duck."

"Who used to call people 'duck'?" I asked.

"I do, and so did my mother," the same lady said.

Later, spirit said, "Duck," again. "Why are you saying it again?" I asked in my mind, and in an instant, I received a vision of a low doorway where one would have to duck!

I said to the woman, "You have a memory of a place with a very low doorway where you would have to crouch to get in."

"Yes," she replied.

Spirit would introduce new symbols from time to time. I noticed that they started saying a lot whenever someone watched a lot of the soap opera Coronation Street. Then they showed me three ducks on the wall, something the recipient would always accept. Now, I have never watched Coronation Street, so it wasn't something that was in my mind. Eventually, I realised that spirit were saying to "get your ducks in a row," i.e. get organised, whenever they showed me this.

I also noticed how spirit people often mentioned that they had enjoyed watching old John Wayne films. This was also always accepted. I know that they are trying to use this as a symbol too, but I am yet to figure that one out!

Getting over Grief & Phillipa's Animals

After my mother passed I had felt very miserable. There came a point where I said to myself, "Enough is enough; I can't be sad anymore; I've felt negative and down for long enough and now I must feel positive!" That evening, a client emailed me that her beloved dog had died. "I will be going home to a quiet house," she said.

Having just pulled myself up by my boots, I didn't want to write a 'poor you' email. Just at the very moment, I had made a decision to be happy, I had received an arrow of sad thoughts directed very innocently at me. So perhaps it was with very bad timing and appeared heartless, but I replied something along the lines of "Don't be sad, you will meet other creatures of pelt and feather!"

Anyway, it turned out to be a prediction, as a few months later, she told me that one morning, she had gone to her kitchen and noticed movement in the courtyard. She looked out, and there was a swan!

Some months later, I visited her to deliver some London garden things to her country home. As was customary, we had a walk around her garden before I headed back to London. As we turned a corner, two swans waddled through an opening in the hedge and walked right up to us. My client was mesmerised, as was I. It was priceless. I suddenly didn't feel so foolish about my earlier comment, and the fact that they made their appearance when I was there was very timely, too.

A few years earlier, this same client's daughter was getting married, and the wedding reception was to be held in a marquee in her country garden. I had done a little work improving the borders and occasionally went to check up on the garden. As the wedding approached, the country gardener was taken ill, so I kept things in order for the approaching big day. Once I went down and I was mesmerised myself, there were two clouds of cabbage white butterflies fluttering over the two rear rose beds. I had planted a tall verbena between the roses, and the butterflies loved that.

The client came out, and we gazed at the sight in front of us together. In my mind's eye, I saw the client's late husband's thick head of hair, which distinguished him. I started to mention it to my client, but she hushed me, deep in thought, I think she was connecting to him too. It was beautiful that he was going to be there for his daughter's wedding. I wonder if he brought along the butterflies as I hadn't seen them there before or since. It was a wonderful sight, and it turned out that his wife's wedding dress had been embroidered with butterflies. It all seemed to tie in.

Watercolours & Fly-Tipping

I woke up one morning from a clear and strong dream about paintings. In the dream, there was a collection of small paintings, which came with the message, "These are valuable!" I realised that my mother was tipping me off!

That day, I had to visit a landscaping job in Islington. This was quite a drive from Kingston, on the other side of London. As I reached Upper Street, I passed an auction house. I had been there before many years ago to buy furniture for my first home in Hackney. "I'm sorry," I sent a thought up to spirit as I drove past without stopping. If the valuable painting is there, I have missed it. I knew that I had not missed anything. In fact, as with a dream like that, one does not need to search. I knew that the painting would present itself to me without me having to do anything.

The next day, I received a text from a guy who I still owed two days' money for gardening work. I was in Putney, and he lived in Mortlake, so I answered that we could meet in Mortlake outside the local garden centre, and we agreed to meet in one hour.

I arrived on time to find him waiting on the pavement, standing in front of a charity shop beside the garden centre. I pulled up my van in front of him and saw, in the window behind him, there was a watercolour painting!

It had presented itself. I paid the guy what I owed him; he gave me an invoice, and then we shook hands and parted. I then darted inside the Charity shop.

I asked the man behind the counter how much the painting in the window was. Fifty pounds was his reply. I did a double take as it wasn't as cheap as I had hoped.

"Will you take less for it?" I ventured, attempting to barter.

The man was a little indignant. "I've done my research," he said, "this is worth a hundred to a hundred and twenty pounds. If I haven't sold it in a couple of weeks, I will drop the price. It only came in yesterday." That clinched it, and I put the fifty pounds onto the counter. It was a quality watercolour, "Yorkshire Storm," by the well-known artist E. Davies, dated 1895.

A few days later, something else remarkable happened in the same area. A staff meeting point was often at Richmond station car park, early in the morning as the guys would meet there before heading off to gardens in west London. I met them there to top up their petty cash and to collect worksheets.

After the meet-up, I thought I would deliver some winter bedding to a garden in Mortlake. It was still early in the morning, and as I turned a corner, there against a building whose entrance was on the street stood nestled against the wall, a Victorian Davenport writing desk. It had been fly-tipped! I did a double-take. I asked myself if it had been stolen and dropped by the thief as he was caught out mid-flight, but no, it had been dumped, nestled neatly against the wall. It was missing a castor, and the leather pad on the sloped writing top wasn't in very good condition. Nevertheless, it was a lovely piece, and I bundled it into my van. I took this as a sign from spirit to pick up a pen!

Dolly Parton & The Psychic Fare

Spirit played a Dolly Parton song in my head. I knew that it was spirit. There was a subtle difference between me humming a song and it coming through from spirit. Sometimes, I would wake up in the morning with a song in my head from spirit. I listened hard, trying to hear the words but couldn't make them out. The next day, another Dolly Parton song came to me, making me wonder if she had passed away! I checked on Google, but she was very much still with us. I gave up, wondering what the meaning was.

It had been two and a half years since my mother had passed to spirit. With Christmas and the winter approaching, my quiet time, and it being Summer in Australia, I had to decide whether to make the journey. "I'll leave it another year before I go," I decided. That was in October. In November, I awoke to a dream that would tell me otherwise.

I was with a client who owned a chain of cinemas. She was playing a home video of her travels, and it was Australian bush. I looked at the film and exclaimed, "That is the bush from the east coast of Tasmania!"

"No, it isn't!" her voice came in the dream. "That is Launceston airport."

I woke up. I thought it strange that I had only just decided not to visit. Ten days later, a letter arrived from my father. He was having an operation, and the worst-case scenario was that an enlarged artery could pop, and he would be dead in an instant. Another ten days passed, and I heard from a sister that he had an operation, and it was a success. I bought my plane ticket.

Another reader reminded me that I had worked spiritually in Tasmania before and that I could work there again. I searched the internet, and as luck would have it, there was a psychic fair in my hometown at the same time that I was visiting. I emailed the organiser, who was more than happy to have me work there.

I arrived on the day of setting up to dress the table. The organiser said we needed a tablecloth, pad, pen and anything else we felt we needed. Some people used crystals and cards. I had bought a bunch of flowers from a roadside stall and dressed the table with these, while the organiser gifted me a candle holder and three candles, one for each day.

"What are the hours?" I asked the organiser as we set up the day before.

"9 to 5," he answered.

The aura photographer standing nearby immediately quipped, "Dolly Parton!"

"Ahh," I thought to myself, spirit had been giving me a sign earlier. Dolly Parton, 9 to 5!

The next day, it was business. People flowed into the hall where it was being held, and before long, I had a reading under my belt. It had gone well, I felt.

At the end of the three days, spirit had touched upon a whole variety of issues, some heavy, including child abuse, family rifts, a son who had not gone to his father's funeral to, the spirit father's disappointment, families who had split up over inheritance disagreements etc.

At the end of each reading, I would ask if there were any questions. One lady asked if she should leave her husband! Another asked if she should go to America, where she could choose the sex of her child, as she only wanted a girl if she were to have another baby.

Another time, a girl wanted to know if the guy she was keen on was the one for her. I explained to all these people that they had to make their own choices in life, and I could not alter their path. I could, however, ask the spirit world and see what they said. Sometimes, they would give me an answer, and sometimes, they would not.

I did ask spirit for these three ladies. Every time, they gave an answer. At times, it was given as a metaphor, and the answer was contained within that. I sent up a thought to spirit about the girl wanting to know if her current boyfriend was "the one." The spirit people took me to a dentist. "I see a cracked tooth." The girl looked at me and muttered, "He is a dentist." We left it at that.

On the second day, spirit came through particularly strongly for a lady. Her mum and dad came through, and they proved themselves. What clinched it was when they talked about a joke to do with a snake.

"Oh," she exclaimed. Back in the day of outhouses, her father had come running out of the toilet with his trousers around his ankles as there was a snake in the outhouse! It had become a family joke. During the reading, spirit said 11/11.

"What does 11/11 mean to you?" I asked.

"Well, that's Remembrance Day," she said.

"Well, it must mean something to you," I pushed because they had said it so clearly. During the reading, the lady had a good cry. Her mum and dad came through so clearly. I wished that all the readings I gave came through so strongly. Then, her spirit people took me to the front door of her house. I had to walk on stepping stones to get to the front door. She confirmed that this was the case at her house. Then, I was shown a large freezer full of food. Now, this is quite a common thing in Australia, but I had to repeat what I was given. The lady confirmed. Now, what is this about? I asked spirit. They immediately answered. "Take the normal steps towards securing your retirement plans, and all will be well. The freezer of food was used as a symbol of her savings, and I understood she had been worried about her investments.

The next day, a woman came to me and said that she felt spirit were trying to get through to her, as everywhere she looked, she saw 11/11! "What does it mean?" she asked me.

"11/11 is Remembrance Day," I said, remembering instantly the message the day before. I felt immediately that spirit had given me the message for the lady the day earlier so that I would have the answer for that day.

The woman explained that she could not forgive herself that her dog had been ill and gone through a lot of pain before she realised that he was ill and had to be put down. I reassured her that the dog was not unwell now in the spirit world. I linked to the dog. I heard a howl.

"You have heard a dog howl recently?" I continued.

"Yes."

"Well, that was the way your dog came through, as it made you think of your dog." She was so pleased to hear from him, as strange as it sounds. I have never had a link to a pet like that before, but I know some people link to their pets more strongly than any human being!

Another girl had come for a reading. Her father came through and said that she had laid her father out. He apologised jokingly for looking so ghoulish. She agreed that she had done the beginnings of laying him out before the undertakers took over. He then showed me the funeral; people were carrying the coffin, but one pallbearer was missing. It made the funeral unbalanced, and her dad was gutted that he hadn't come.

"That's right," the woman said and explained her brother had not attended. I made a note to myself to attend the funerals of all my major relatives despite the distance! Spirit also showed me symbolically a homemade see-saw made from a plank of wood on a barrel. "There was somebody with a drink problem..."

"Yes."

"You tried your best to keep them level."

"Yes," she agreed.

"But they were up and down."

Later in the reading, spirit put in my mind that there had been child abuse in the family. My heart sank. I broached the subject as sensitively as I could. The lady accepted the information immediately, and I could see that she had dealt with it.

"It was my sister," she said. "She became an alcoholic and then committed suicide." The lady in spirit hadn't got that far yet, but she did say how cunning the abuser had been to get away with it. "Yes," the lady agreed.

The woman in the spirit world had simply not been able to cope and had turned to drink, which in turn led to suicide.

The woman explained at the end that she had given up her job to look after her father through his illness. The surviving brother and sister had agreed that it was ok for her to get all of the inheritance, of which there wasn't much, she said. On her father's death, the two children turned on the sister, who had given up everything to look after him. The brother had not gone to his father's funeral, and they hadn't spoken since! Spirit told this lady she should not let life pass her by and mentioned a first kiss. Her life was about to turn around after all of her struggles. She had a very well-deserved new future waiting for her!

At the psychic fair, not being used to working nine to five for spirit, I was concerned that I might run out of energy making the connections. All the other nine readers, bar one, read using cards. I never read cards. There were an array for sale on one of the stalls. I immediately felt drawn to a pack of animal cards. The first day, I didn't look at them once.

On the second day, I asked the recipient to shuffle the cards and draw three she felt drawn to. I took them face down and proceeded with the reading. With this particular lady, I asked if she had a picture of a tiger at home. "Yes," she said, "I drew it!"

At the end of the reading, I turned over the first card. It was a tiger! We laughed about that. I didn't read the message on the card, which was written below the animal, but instead looked at the card to see what I could pick out of it. The cards were a focus. It could have been the colours around it that I felt drawn to, not necessarily the animal itself.

Another lady pulled three cards; this time, it was my turn to be surprised. She pulled a picture of a spider upon a web. I read the caption below. This card represented creativity. When I worked clairvoyantly in the past, whenever I saw a spider on a web in my mind's eye, it was the sign for creativity! I had linked into the collective consciousness to get this symbol!

Truganini & Bruny Island

After the snake and Truganini experience in Exeter, I wanted to visit Truganini's homeland. She was from the Oyster Bay Tribe, and they lived on Bruny Island, a twenty-minute ferry journey from the Tasmanian mainland. While in Tasmania, I asked my sister if she wanted to go on a holiday there, and she was very happy to accompany me. My old school friend Chris recommended I go to a natural, freestanding stone arch on a beach there. He explained that in 1953, Queen Elizabeth and Prince Philip had moored the royal yacht Britannia off the coast there on the way from Sydney to Hobart. Then the royal party had taken a smaller boat to that very spot and had a picnic under the stone arch. Chris 'Google Earthed' it for me, Grace booked an Airbnb, I sorted the car hire out, and my father lent me a sat nav. We were all prepared!

My favourite route was to turn off the highway at Deloraine, head further inland, and drive up the western tiers and over the central plateau. It was there, years earlier, that I had felt Jesus visit me and talk about forgiveness. Another time, with my mother and sister, we saw three echidnas, anteaters, walking by the roadside in three separate places. I thought it was special up there, and the alpine vegetation was always nice to see. As we reached the top, there was a car park with a wooden walkway leading through an ancient King William pine thicket that led to a lake.

We stopped there and walked the track. As we came back, another car parked up with its radio blaring. I greeted the driver, seeing he had a stubby of beer beside the handbrake.

"Mienas closed," he said.

The bush fire was nearby. We heeded his advice and turned back. Halfway down the mountain, we took a gravel road to Cressy, a small farming town. Then, we continued on the countryside route closer to the base of the tiers before joining the highway.

We reached Kettering at 5pm and caught the car ferry across. We were halfway over when I spotted something in the water ahead. Were they black swans? Was it a fishing cage? As we neared the objects, I was delighted to see they were seals with their flippers in the air! I thought it was a welcoming committee! We disembarked and drove to the south of the island. The north and south are divided by a long and narrow neck of land. Halfway along, there was a lookout. This was named Truganini Lookout in her honour.

We stopped and walked to the top. We had marvellous views of the neck, and to the left and right of the lookout stretched a vast arc of a beach several miles long. This was called Adventure Bay. In the far distance, I saw the rocky outcrop that broke the far end of the beach up. Beyond this must be the arch that Chris spoke of.

We drove on and found the B & B before driving back to have supper at the Bruny Island Hotel, where my sister had wallaby lasagne, and I had wallaby spring rolls!

On our full day, we started with a boat ride, seeing some incredible wildlife, including dolphins and a shy albatross. I remember spirit calling me an albatross when I visited my mother so frequently. The scenery was majestic as well, with amazing caves, a blowhole called the 'breathing stone', and rock pillars rising out of the sea and looking like they had come straight off the set of Lord of the Rings. All this is described entertainingly by the boat's commentary.

Back on dry land, we went back to Truganini's Lookout before setting off for the distant rock cliff in search of the stone arch. There was plenty to look at as we walked along; seaweed, shells, and even a message in a bottle, but it had been written just two days before at Port Arthur. It was all good fun!

We must have walked for two hours before we neared the cliffs. The tide was coming in, and the waves were lapping around the rocks, which meant we couldn't get to the arch, which was somewhere beyond the rocks. I gazed at the cliff, and suddenly, I had a vision: the cliff had turned into the Sphinx. I blinked, and I saw the Sphinx overlay the cliff again.

"Are my eyes playing tricks on me?" I muttered to myself.

"What? "My sister asked who was stood beside me.

"Oh, it's nothing," I replied.

We approached the cliff, now back to simply being a cliff, just as a cyclist came up from behind.

"Excuse me," I said, "are you local?"

"Yes," he panted.

"Is there a stone arch here?"

"Yes," he replied and pointed to an opening set further back into the cliff. This was a pass through the cliff! Chris hadn't mentioned this, and I couldn't believe our luck.

"Is there another arch?"

"Yes, it's another 200 meters along."

I thanked him, and we made our way. As I looked up at the arch, I glimpsed a statue of Buddha in its rocky surface. I blinked. The Buddha appeared fleetingly again. We went on through the arch. It was so beautiful there. Much of Tasmania is pristine and scenic. The air is the freshest in the world, and the seas are clean and clear. I filled my lungs, breathing in this pureness. A Sphinx and then Buddha. What was the connection?

We found the arch and had a well-deserved rest, my sister taking the opportunity to have a smoke. It was such a wonderful place. Then we set off back to Truganini Lookout.

The next time I had some quiet time alone to ponder, I concluded that it was spirit guides, one Egyptian and one Buddhist, making themselves known to me. Like with my trip to India, after hearing Mrs Durga's voice when my mother died, and not feeling Mrs Durga with me when I was there, I did not feel Truganini or my mum with me on Bruny Island. It didn't matter. It was an amazing island. It was so peaceful, and I felt it held a healing energy. It was also great to spend time with my sister.

Back in London & Serving Churches

Back in London and another service at Morden. One lady got the longest message by far, and I could tell from the information that was given to her that she needed it!

A lady in spirit said that she had gone to Lourdes to be healed.

"Yes," she said.

"But it didn't work," I continued and went back to spirit.

"You know somebody whose name is Bernadette?" I asked, before adding, "She is not well."

"Yes," the woman replied.

My own mind immediately came into it, as I knew that the Saint of Lourdes was named Bernadette! I went back to the lady in spirit and asked what's next. She replied that she had contacted Saint Bernadette in the spirit world and was sending healing to the Bernadette that she knew! I was amazed by this.

When I started to work, I wouldn't know who I would be going to, so I always asked spirit to give me something to start with. On this particular morning, after the opening prayer, hymns, reading, address, and healing prayer, the time came for the clairvoyance. I threw my mind up to the spirit world. The reply came back: "Mention Captain Birdseye fish fingers!"

I hesitated, and then, knowing that it was from spirit and that I was not to doubt it, I gave a message to two ladies sitting behind each other. One lady could accept it! Well, a piece of information like that was certainly unique!

Starting on a fresh connection, the spirit people gave me a hamster on a hamster wheel.

"Who had a hamster on a wheel as a child?" I threw out. Four people raised their hands.

I went back to spirit and asked for the next piece of information. They showed me a snake in a glass tank! And then the frozen mice that it was fed. "Ugh," I thought. Ok, I will say it.

"Who here can understand a pet snake?" Two of the four people understood the information. Again, I threw my mind up. I couldn't believe what they gave me! There was a theme going on here! One of the two ladies had a memory of keeping a pet spider. I relayed it, and I was then down to one lady. I proceeded with her message.

A gentleman came through, he said he had a family in life who had abandoned him. The recipient, his mother-in-law, I found out later, agreed with that. The man went on to say that it was actually a good thing to be abandoned as it provided the abandoned one a chance to express himself fully. His family were very restrictive and would not allow him to follow his own dreams. He begrudged them when he was alive, but when he passed, he could see that it was actually a good thing in his case!

I was working at a church in Walton when I saw a man holding a motorbike beside the lady I was reading for. I told her this, and she acknowledged him. Suddenly, the floor in front of me opened up, and a man's head popped out of the floor! Of course, this was in my mind's eye, but as it was external clairvoyance, it was the last thing I expected to see.

"Did you know a man who worked in the drains?" I asked.

"Yes," she replied, "my dad, he died five days ago." This shocked me, of course, and I suddenly thought I needed to be very careful what I said, as the woman was so recently bereft. This broke the link.

I was at a psychic fair, and it was so quiet that we started to give each other readings. I was in mid-flow with one particular lady.

"I see pink around you."

"No," she said, "I don't normally like pink." Then, after a pause, she continued, "Well, I did paint my nails pink recently." She flashed me her nails. In my mind's eye, I saw a little girl dressed in pink.

"There is a little girl in spirit world," I told her.

"No," came the reply, which quickly went to an "OMG yes, my

neighbours lost their daughter, and it was her anniversary on the weekend, so I gave them a card, and it was filled with pink stars."

"She is influencing you," the little girl reminded me.

"Gosh, I've put something pink in my hall, and I never ever go for that colour."

"It is because she has been drawing close," I said. She is in your energy, and so she is influencing yours. As she draws close, the things that she liked in life are subtly influencing your mind, and so you have been inspired to add pink to your life!"

About a week later, I was at a church, and somebody else drew close and said, "Have you noticed how you have started looking for a bargain and you never used to? You get excited over a 'two for one' deal.

"Yes," the recipient said.

"Well, that's because the person who liked a bargain is drawing close. She is influencing you just by being in your aura."

The spirit world was teaching me. My mind drew back to when I thought I had done something out of my usual character. It was the influence of spirit. I had that as a child with the spirits of the Tasmanian aborigines. I would daydream about living in the bush or when I wanted to sink a path in my mother's garden.

Another few weeks followed, and I had an evening of clairvoyance in a St. John's Ambulance hall in Chertsey, run by a very spiritual lady, Barbara. There was a lovely atmosphere, with a group of very down-to-earth, jolly people!

I sat in the front row and opened up whilst I was waiting for it to begin. I was given the customary cup of tea. I looked across, and standing beside Barbara was Tony Gates! He was a gardening customer of mine who had died a few years earlier. "What are you doing here?" I thought to him. But I knew in an instant that he was here to help. I saw him so clearly.

Barbara called me up to the chair and I sat across from her with a table in the middle. Some 25 people were there. We sang a hymn, I opened in prayer, and another hymn, and then I was introduced. I gave my usual short talk and started. I just heard the word "April", that was all. I asked if anybody could understand the significance of April. Either a name or the month. A long silence ensued! The board behind us gave a loud crack, and we knew that there was spirit about. I still didn't get anything else, so I went back to Tony.

"Barbara, you know a Tony in the spirit world?"

"Yes," she said, and we were off. The words tumbled out, and there were many people there for Barbara. The Tony I knew had drawn close to give me his name, and I thanked him with my mind. The evening was a success. For another lady, a white pony came through. She accepted the horse immediately, and then, to my surprise, a Shetland pony came through. She accepted him, too. The funny thing to me was that the Shetland was so bad-tempered and had a real attitude. The women accepted that, too! There was some unusual evidence as the evening went on.

As usual, over the following few days, I saw some things that had been given as a reading. The strangest was that I had told a lady that she had a cloth with a Dalmatian print on it. To my amazement, she said yes! "That's a bit random," I thought. Grace, at the office a week later, was wearing a green dress with Dalmatian dog prints on it. Another example was on the back of a truck when I was stuck in traffic. There was a picture of a tiger, and I had said to one of the ladies in the audience that she would randomly see pictures or images of tigers.

I chuckled, as I also saw a tiger later in the day as I drove home and stopped at some traffic lights. A large buxom lady had walked in front of my van and was wearing a top with the face of a tiger on it. The funny thing was that each of the tiger's eyes was in the middle of her bosoms!

Later in the evening, when it finished, a lady who had received a nice message came up to me and told me that she had three husbands, and they were all born in April. She didn't want to accept it, she said, because she didn't want to hear from any of them!

It was one of the best evenings I had taken for a long time. I think it was simply because they were such a friendly group of people with a good attitude that spirit could come through so easily.

Chapter Thirteen

WHITE MAGIC

I went to a last-minute weekday service as a replacement medium, as the original one had needed to pull out at the last minute. I arrived and was put in a quiet room to open up. I tried to, but instead drifted off to sleep! I think spirit guides were priming me in my sleep.

I went into the church hall, and unusually, it was filled with about 30 people, which was a lot for a spiritual church. Of course, it is not just about numbers, but the atmosphere can be sharper then. We went through the usual formalities of an opening prayer and a song; then it was handed over to me.

I explained that, more often than not, I didn't know who the message was for and that any recipient should speak up if they understood the information while at the same time being sure not to 'feed' the medium with information.

I said that sometimes the information came through loud and clear, and at other times, the spirit seemed far away. I asked that the congregation have an open mind and send me love and support. I paused, sent my thoughts up to spirit, and waited for a response. All of a sudden, I felt stuck in a lift.

"Who here has been stuck in a lift?" I asked to be greeted by a long and deafening silence.

"I don't mind how long ago this was, "I said encouragingly.

A single hand meekly arose. "Ah, you can understand that", I stated matter-of-factly. "Then I am with you. I don't know who I have here, but let's see."

I retook my energy up to the spirit world. "Show me the next thing," I asked with my mind. I didn't see a person; I saw a deer and a stag, then it changed into an antelope, and I saw many African animals.

"Can you understand African animals?" I asked. "Or can someone around you understand this?"

"I am from North Africa," the same woman answered.

"Excellent," I said. The visions increased, and her father came through and proved himself.

I was conscious that I seemed to stay with this lady for a long time, well over 20 minutes. I tried to move on, but knowing from past experience, I could only move on once spirit had said what they wanted. It would have been akin to hanging up halfway through a telephone conversation.

I only went to 4 people in the dem. Eventually, I felt my energy drop, and no spirit present. I asked the chair if it was ok if I finished. The evening had gone on for 90 minutes. Spirit chooses who is going to get the message, not the medium. Another medium told me that spirit had it all worked out before the evening had even begun. I can well believe that.

Speaking without a script can be daunting, so I often repeated this to myself before a service to remind myself that I just had to do my bit and that it was all planned out in advance. Spirit would never let me down. I just had to be there for them.

"You understand the name, Mary," a medium said to me. I couldn't think of any Marys, so I said nothing. About ten days later, I was walking to Morden to serve the church there. As I neared, I felt a spirit person draw close. They drew closer and closer until suddenly I knew who it was: Mary Armour! She was delighted that I recognised her, and I thanked her so much for drawing close. She was full of joy. How apt, I thought. She loved mediumship, and I knew she was there to watch me work. I kicked myself for not recognising her name earlier.

I'm sorry to say that I received a Grenfell Message. Grenfell was the London tower block that had burned due to the flammable cladding catching alight and where many innocent souls had lost their lives. The morning after, I was on my way to a roof garden, and we passed very close by, with the flames still ablaze and the smoke rising into the city sky. It was an awful sight.

About a month later, I was with a friend. We were driving on the Westway, which is a raised highway taking people in and out of London to the west and passes quite close to the now burnt-out tower block. My colleague started to tell me how an Italian girl trapped at the top of the building had called her family in Italy.

"Stop!" I cried out; I couldn't hear this story. I felt a connection.

Arriving at Morden for one of my biannual services, there was a smattering of people in the congregation. The service started in the usual way, and after the first message, I sent my mind up for the next one. I saw firehoses and a man holding one.

I have a fireman here, I said, waiting for someone to accept him. Nobody answered, and I was about to move on when a woman said, "You might be with me; I know a fireman." With that, a group energy of souls drew very close, and I started to channel word for word.

"How can you feel so guilty? You did all that you could. You didn't even know us, but you put yourself in great danger. You did all that you could, and we are grateful to you for that. You showed great bravery."

It turned out that the lady's daughter's friend was a fireman who had fought the Grenfell blaze. He was not in a good way, and he felt dreadful that he had been unable to save people whom he had been very close to saving, but ultimately could not because of the heat.

I met the lady again some six months later at a different church. They had told the fireman the message, and he could understand it. It went some way to helping him heal from his ordeal.

A Visit to Hungary

Another busy summer had passed, and I had only snatched two long weekends off. Desperate to hire some trustworthy, hardworking staff, I emailed Peter, who had now settled back in his homeland of Hungary, to raise a family. He responded with a possibility and asked when I was going to visit.

I went the next weekend, knowing that if I didn't do it then, I would never get around to it. The change of scenery and company was welcome, and it was great to catch up. Peter and Monica, his wife, had both become teachers. The area was mainly inhabited by gypsies, and eighty per cent of the students were gypsy children. The first day, we went to a gypsy village for a football match. Peter played every Saturday and was one of the few not from gypsy descent.

On the second day, we headed off for a morning at a thermal bath and then went to the highest point in Hungary, at 1064 metres above sea level. On the way to the mountain, we saw a ruined castle on the hill approaching. We decided to go, as we had plenty of time.

We followed the signposts and ended up at the car park at the foot of the hill in the village of Sirkol. We walked up to the castle, following the path as it hugged the hillside. A few broken walls remained, but nothing else except a well, some rooms carved out of the stone, and an underground network of tunnels.

Further up, some roughly hewn stone steps led into a raised cave. This was intriguing as it turned out to be a labyrinth. I turned on my iPhone's torch, but before long, shafts of light appeared down the passageways from windows and a stairwell to the upper level of the castle. This was a great lookout, and we surveyed the views.

Before descending, I spotted another staircase going down into another tunnel. I thought it would link up to the others, so we followed it down.

At the bottom, there were some very worn stone steps. There was a hole in the hillside, and one could look out onto the countryside. As we reached it, some stones fell from a hole above. "Tourists," Peter said.

"A ghost," I replied, raising my eyebrows, teasing.

It turned out that these tunnels went nowhere, so we went back to the summit and descended to the lower level, where there was an exhibit of artefacts and artists' impressions of what the castle had once looked like. Eventually, we took our leave and, after returning to the car, headed onward to the summit.

Unlike many countries' highest place, this one was far from remote. It had tourist trinket stalls, a restaurant and, sadly, a shrine to those killed in motorcycle accidents there in Hungary. There was also a tall antenna with satellite dishes for TV, telephone, and goodness knows what else. One thing the structure did have was a cafeteria about seven floors up, so we headed for that to enjoy the views.

Impulsively, I took the stairs rather than the lift! "Why have I done this?" I thought.

The stairs were endless. Just as I was regretting my decision with aching legs, we reached the viewing platform. The views over the beech-tree-covered mountain and beyond were glorious. Peter said he would not have followed me, apart from the fact that he didn't want to lose his guest.

Suddenly, Peter grabbed my arm. "Look," he exclaimed. I followed to where my friend was pointing. Cloud covered the surrounding countryside apart from one tiny break that shone a shaft of sunlight directly onto Sirkol! The ruined castle stood out alone in the entire landscape, like a beacon. What were the chances of that? The ghost, or should I say the spirit of Peter's father, had been there earlier, and that was my proof. I didn't say anything to Peter about it. As his father had spoken to me some years earlier, as he was leaving this mortal coil, and now, here was a miracle. Peter is a sensitive soul, and I knew he found the synchronicity significant. If we had taken the lift, we would have missed the sight.

Fun Fairs

The end of the year was approaching, and with that came the third fair that I was booked to do. I arrived to set out my stall, which involved laying out a cloth, a few crystals, and cards, to find I was supposed to give a public demonstration along with another medium.

I only had minutes to open up and no time to get nervous, but of course, nerves still managed to creep in. We had about 40 minutes between us, and the other medium said she wanted to go first.

My colleague started and read a lot of people very quickly. She seemed to go over her time, and as she wrapped it up and left, half of the audience left with her! I wondered if they realised, I was on next! I thought this was my lucky break. I gave a very brief introduction and began. Spirit immediately showed me a volcano.

"There is someone in the spirit world who lived within sight of a volcano," I stated and looked out over the sea of faces.

There was an awkward silence. I knew what I had received, so I added, I don't mind how long ago this was, but I know that somebody lived within sight of a volcano.

A lady piped up that her grandparents lived in Naples and could see Vesuvius from their house.

"There we are," I said, relieved. "Now, a volcano is always a symbol of a blow-up in a family, and I know that there has been a blow-up around you, and I want to sidestep the fallout." The lady agreed.

The nice thing about working for non-church people is that they seem so amazed by any accuracy! I said to the lady, "We are claiming to work for spirit, so we should not be incorrect. Spirit are always right, so don't be so surprised!"

Spirit then gave me the name of her daughter. Then they mentioned doctors.

"Oh yes," she said, "there is a long line of doctors in my family."

I laughed and told her how spirit had given me the information. "It's funny," I told her, as they showed me a skeleton, like you see in a doctor's surgery." The reading went on. I've never liked giving a negative reading, but after the volcano, spirit also talked about an aunt with a handbag made out of crocodile skin.

"Somebody around you has been snappy," I said. Other things came through. The lady seemed so amazed by the information. I only went to one other lady as I was out of time, and I wound the presentation up.

As had happened so very many times, I saw things that I had given in the reading the following week. One evening, I walked into the local tapas bar opposite my office, and they had a full-size skeleton, just the same as I had seen for the lady as part of their Halloween decorations.

At my next church service, I clearly saw a picture of Amy Winehouse. The recipient's mother and granddaughter were both called Amy. I went back to Amy and asked what she wanted to say, as she was still there so strongly. I felt drawn to her hair. It turned out that the lady's granddaughter wore her hair in the same style. She had come along so much out of the blue, and obviously, as a well-known name, she had made an impression on me.

At one point in my gardening work, I employed Matthew, Luke, and John. I thought to myself, now all I need is Mark. At the next service, spirit put this same thought into my mind as I linked to a chap in the audience. I reeled off these three names. The chap laughed. "My name is Mark," he said. Spirit was having a joke.

A week later, I was demming at Richmond Spiritualist Church. My job had been stressful that week with my day job. I was adamant that I would not stress about anything or anybody at church. As a result, I was unusually laid back. The evening went well, and the messages flowed.

I like it when spirit drop something in front of me. When I was giving a reading this particular evening in Richmond, I was giving a message, and spirit said in the middle of it, "Linda."

"Who's Linda," I asked.

"My sister," the lady in the audience replied.

"This is relevant to your sister." Then, as I carried on, they showed me a horseshoe on the wall facing down, as they sometimes are.

"You will remember where the horseshoe was on the wall."

"Yes," she replied immediately.

"You have been feeling unlucky of late, as the horseshoe is facing down, so your luck is pouring out," I explained. "Well, spirit have turned the horseshoe around the other way, so know that your luck is changing and spirit have a hand in it."

She thanked me, and the messages went on. I worked until I felt spirit draw away, and my 'spiritual battery' was low.

The very next day, I had a meeting with a garden designer whom I had worked with several times before. Her garden designs were always great, and her approach was lovely, so I was looking forward to the meeting.

This was in a very smart part of central London. We entered the refurbishment, a Regency semi-detached villa that was very much a building site, with the two-storey site office taking up much of the garden.

As we went to leave and I was hanging up hard hats and high-vis jackets, which we had to wear to comply with health and safety; there, beside the door, propped up by two screws, was a horseshoe. I remembered my reading immediately.

Spirit were making a change in my own fortune.

Gandhi

Another dem, this time at Barnes Healing Church. The first connection came through, much of which was accepted, stories of bombings during the war. A hot water bottle was mentioned: "I've just bought one as a Christmas present!" She said. The connection seemed to fluctuate.

The second connection came along. "Francis," spirit stated.

"He is my doctor," the man said. I went back into the ether, asking for more information. A guy came through who looked remarkably like Gandhi, but I didn't want to be pompous and say I have Gandhi here! The recipient was also slim and Indian.

"Where your people came from, it was hot, and they didn't have to wear many clothes," I said, describing the Gandhi-like man in a loincloth.

"Yes, that's right," the recipient responded encouragingly.

I edged forward. "Do you understand a man like this who was thin, bald and didn't wear much?"

"No!" the man answered.

I still had the vision of Gandhi in front of me. Clairsentiently, I was beside the Ganges. I felt it very strongly and had been there myself, to Varanasi. "Have you been to the Ganges?" I asked.

"No," he replied again.

"One day, you will go to the Ganges," I told him.

"Not likely," was his reply. I felt deflated. Then he added, "But I will write it in my will that I want to have my ashes scattered over the Ganges!"

"Well, you will get there, one way or another." This man was going to the Ganges! Everybody laughed.

The third person got a message, and I talked about writing books, which she accepted. She mentioned that the Gandhi guy and her had written and published books. These were about spirituality, and one was about Gandhi himself. I realised then that I had, in fact, seen Gandhi.

A lady in a sari drew close. "You knew an Indian lady now in the spirit world?"

"Yes."

"She wore beautiful saris."

"Yes."

The lady in spirit started to rub the fabric of her sari.

"You are good with cloth," I said, "and cloth of quality."

"That was my job for 15 years."

"Well, you may find that you go back to it in some capacity," I told her.

For the next person, spirit started with the name of Ruth. Then added aunty.

"Yes," he said.

I was surprised that spirit were starting off with names.

"Well, somebody has been crying on your shoulder," I said.

"Yes, that's right."

"You know where somebody keeps turning the heating up, and another comes along and turns it down."

"Yes."

Spirit were drawing on my own experience; my new office person was from Lebanon and loved the office hot. He kept turning it up, and I kept turning it down. I liked it cold and was always mindful of the electricity bills.

It was a good night.

An Electric Shock & Coloured Skies

I had mentioned to an old friend that I could do with a break. She said that I should ask her parents if I could stay at their holiday villa in Italy, as not only did they love it when people stayed there, but they were also friends of mine.

Had the daughter not suggested it, I would have felt it would have been too cheeky to ask. But ask I did, and they very kindly said yes.

I mentioned a break to one of the readers, and she said that I would have spiritual experiences. I didn't like being told that as it set up an expectation. Anyway, I went with an open mind.

I arrived in Genoa to pouring rain. I followed the written instructions faithfully on how to get to the villa, which was in a coastal town. My mind was a bit addled by the time I got there, and I ended up at the villa with the key, unable to get in, though I had followed the instructions to the letter! It was still raining heavily, so I backtracked to a hotel I had passed and stayed the night there comfortably. I thought I would try the villa one more time when I was thinking straight, and it wasn't in the middle of a downpour.

To cut a long story short, I managed to contact the local agent who was looking after the villa, and I met them there. It turned out that I was trying the wrong villa, though weirdly, the night before, a key into the wrong villa had opened the gate!

I settled down to unwind, read books, eat good food and go for long walks. I went back to the train station and got a train to the next town, where I could get a ferry to a monastery. The three-hour walk back to the nearest village was magical. At one point, the energy changed, and there was a waterfall, like in Tasmania. I thought I saw a dog ahead, which turned out to be a wild boar. Luckily, it turned out not to be too wild as I walked past a group of five of them, and they didn't mind me one bit. I went into a natural high, so content to be in nature. I wondered if this was the spiritual experience that had been foretold.

The day after, I ventured into the town and beyond to the main church, the Church of St James. Next to this was a garden and the grand old 18th-century Villa Sainta Margeuretta, which was open to the public.

After visiting the church, I walked into the classically Italian garden and approached the villa. I must have been halfway along the garden when, and this is the only way I can think to describe it, I walked through an energy field. I received a mild electric shock! There must be a veil of protection around the villa, I thought. I went into the villa for a tour, thinking I may get some insight into my experience, or perhaps see a spirit person.

I ventured in with an open mind. It was great wandering around, imagining what the place would have been like in times past. The energy field experience was soon forgotten, and I just enjoyed being nosey! As I came out, the sun was setting with a pink sky. I took some photos of the beautiful garden and another looking back to Saint James with the pink sky.

At the end of the three-and-a-half-hour walk back, I thought I would send some photos of my holiday to my sister, who had come so strongly into my mind whilst I was walking. I sent a selection. Within seconds, I received a text message from this sister. It was a photo of a pink sky, and beneath it was the name, address, and phone number of my other sister. She had just had her 60th birthday a few weeks earlier. This was my sister's way of making the point that I had gone on holiday but not to a birthday party on the other side of the world. I was furious.

A month later, I was on the phone having a reading, and the lady said, "Your mother is showing me photos. It's spiritual. There is a pink sky!"

"Ah, amazing," I said. I know that photo, but it is not spiritual. My sister used it as a way of saying I should have flown around the world for a birthday party.

"No, it is spiritual", the reader insisted.

Suddenly, the penny dropped. "Actually, yes," I said, I walked through an energy field where I took the photo of the pink sky. I thought it was a ring of protection for the villa, but she said that spirit were adjusting my energy. Gosh, amazing, I thought. I wouldn't have known it was that unless I phoned for a reading.

There was my spiritual experience, which had been foretold, and I had discounted it! I was told that they would 'step me up'.

A Special Reading

I was working at a fair. The lady who ran it also offered free one-hour events to attendees in an adjacent hall. I took advantage of the offer and gave a talk and demonstration. There was good energy there, which resulted in good connections.

Afterwards, I went to the stall alongside the other readers, offering my services for private readings. A lady came to me who had been at the talk but not had a message. I explained what I did, and we settled down for the reading. I held out my hands to hold hers to strengthen the link. I got a few things that she accepted, and then after a few minutes, I said that there was a girl in spirit. The information flowed. The tears flowed, more from me than this lady.

In my first circle, the teacher had advised me to never cry with the sitter, as you cannot help them if you descend into that emotion. In this case, the tears were the lady's tears; I felt her buried pain.

Her daughter came through stronger and stronger. The lady blamed herself in some way for her daughter's passing, which was through an illness. She went on to say that she had been taken elsewhere to see if something could be done or for another opinion. The tears streamed down both of our faces at this point.

"You are not to blame yourself," came through, which I obviously passed on.

"That means a lot," the woman said. Her pain was so raw. She still had school clothes with her name sewn into it.

All sorts of evidence came through. As soon as the reading came to an end, the tears stopped. I went to the toilet for a wash and thought I wouldn't be able to read for anyone else that day, as after all that emotion, I was a little taken aback. A little while later, however, my energy bounced back, and feeling more like my normal self again, I went back to the table. The woman's partner, who was not the child's father, then asked for a reading.

"I'm interested; how long ago did your partner lose her daughter?" I asked him as we settled down at the table.

"Seven years ago," he replied. I couldn't believe it. This poor lady had lived in such great pain and torment for seven years. I had assumed it had happened one or two years before. I felt that I had been in the right place at just the right time to help this lady to take the first steps to a much-needed healing path.

A cousin in Australia had suffered a severe asthma attack, which put her into a coma. After several months, she slipped away to the spirit world. During the reading, everything I told this lady was about my cousin. It was as though my cousin was feeding me with the information as it was completely relevant to this lady.

As I said, I was the right person in the right place at the right time for this lady, albeit for sad reasons. I know I helped her take one step in the right direction. Her partner had been very worried about her.

This reading, along with the one where the man said, "When you touch the angel, I feel you," will always stay with me.

Running A Circle

I was sat at my office desk with my day job. I felt Derek Robinson draw close. "What are you saying?" I asked. I couldn't decipher the reply if one did indeed come back. That night, I had a dream about somebody from the church. She ran a circle to the best of my knowledge.

The next day, I sent a message to Derek's grandson, Ashley, asking if there were any openings to run a circle. "Yes," he replied straight away. "Ahh, I thought," I was right in interpreting the dream. After some short negotiations, I was booked to run a teaching circle, my first. "You must be psychic, as we were looking for a circle leader," Ashley joked.

The first class had three people and, although few in number, went well enough. The next class was up to seven. We had agreed a 10-week course to be held fortnightly. Usually, I would set the class members a little homework. One such lot was to observe any occurrences where we felt spirit influence our day-to-day lives.

At the class, we went around for people to share. The stories were varied and all amazing in their own way. A lady, Anne, shared that she had been on a walk with her partner, where they had passed a Hindu temple. They had admired the stone carving on the outside before continuing on their walk. Sometime later, the couple came to a canal, and as they made their way along the towpath, they saw some council workers dredging the waterway. There was a pile of rubbish beside what they had fished out of the canal. Anne spotted a small mud-covered statue of Ganesh. Having earlier walked beside the Hindu temple, she felt it was a significant find, and after asking the workers if she could take it, she took it home, gave it a wash and sat it on her mantelpiece.

I said to Anne, well, if you feel that is significant and spirit-influenced, so be it. I didn't think it was that remarkable, as it sounded like the Hindu temple wasn't that far away.

The next day at work, I went to see some of the gardeners working for me. It was lunchtime, and they were sat in the van having lunch. Sat on the van's dashboard was a mascot of a small Ganesh statue! Spirit are backing up Anne, I thought! I took a picture of the Ganesh and sent it to the circle's WhatsApp group. It felt like we had our own miracle!

The energy at Clapham Church was always very spiritual, and I shouldn't say it, but I thought I always worked well there! I started to take monthly workshops. The numbers swelled to ten, and it was a great group. Some of the people had amazing abilities, and they were all so keen and enthusiastic. It was refreshing to be around such people, and it was a success. I was a bit nervous, but having Argentina there, who was a medium herself, was a great help and support.

I drew on exercises that I had learnt when I was a student. Before I left home for one session, I had pulled out my photo album, carefully removed a picture of my mother, put it in an envelope, and sealed it. Then, as I drove to Clapham, I realised I had not asked my mother for permission if people could link into her energy. I sent a thought of request up.

When I was around 14 or 15, my mother and I had taken a trip to the mainland to visit her people. My uncle, who had inherited the family farm, took us to the 'out farm', another piece of land the family-owned, which had an old brick homestead, now a ruin. The picture in the envelope was one I took of my mother looking through one of the homestead's large windows back towards me. I guess I was trying to be artistic at the time.

Everyone in the circle held the envelope and were asked to link to the person in the picture. Afterwards, I went around one by one and asked the people what they got.

One man described a wooden veranda, an upstairs barn door and wide-open spaces. As my mother was from the Wheatbelt part of Victoria in Australia, it was certainly open space, and the second family home in which my mother was brought up had a wooden veranda and a barn on the other side of the farmyard. The hairs stood up on my arms as the next person said, "I see a boy looking through a window!"

Well, of course, that was me taking the photo, although I was not in the photo myself. Apart from that, I could not really accept much from the others. It was a very interesting exercise. We did some other more typical exercises of people pairing up and swapping readings, firstly with people of similar abilities, then later on, I put a more advanced person with a beginner, and this seemed to work a lot better. There was a girl in the class who I deduced later in the day that she was on antidepressants. "You shouldn't really be here today," I told her, but I hadn't pushed her to work, and I know she received an incredibly healing message from a talented student.

Later in the day, we did a guided meditation. When we came 'back down to earth,' I felt really spaced out. As the girl on the antidepressants was beside me, I realised I had absorbed her energies empathically.

We did another exercise where I would pick out somebody to face the wall. They would link to the spirit world and then share the message that they received. Nobody else could answer except by shaking or nodding their heads. I was the mouthpiece and would confirm if the information was correct. The students were amazingly good at this, and I was shocked.

I tried this again with my circle, and we were all rubbish, myself included!

I took a service at Walton Spiritualist Church. There was a good atmosphere, and it was well attended. At this church, the chairperson sat on the platform, and the medium had a chair directly in front of the congregation. I felt exposed, not having anything to sit behind.

It was a good evening, and the energy flowed. I noticed that spirit borrowed some information from a previous evening: you were stuck in a lift. I was in the middle of a reading to one lady, and a man in what I thought was an Air Force uniform flashed in front of me.

"You know of a man in the family who was in the Air Force," I said.

"No," the lady answered.

"Oh," I thought, perhaps I didn't see it clearly. I tried again. "You must know a man in the family in the navy then."

"No," she said again. I was puzzled as although he didn't stay long, I knew what I had seen, and he had shown me himself clearly.

"Well, I'll tell you what I saw," I said, "a man in a blue uniform, and he had three stripes on his shoulder."

"I don't know," the woman answered honestly.

I stood in the energy. The man then gave me a vibe. "You know somebody with their pilot's license?"

"Oh yes," she said, "a friend."

I stood again in the energy. "He has followed in the footsteps of another."

"Yes, his grandfather."

The man stepped forward again. "Ahh!" I exclaimed; it was the man I had seen earlier. I went back to him. He was very emotional, and there was a great feeling of pride. He was all choked up. He was so proud of his grandson, who had followed in his footsteps.

"We were all proud of him," the lady said, "as he was particularly young when he got it."

I was pleased to get a message for someone who was not even there and not in this lady's family. The man had proved himself. It was a good night.

Firing Sergio

Years earlier, I had a reading from a lady and spirit said, "We are not going to help you with a particular relationship." I took it on the chin and carried on pursuing the relationship. Needless to say, nothing came of it!

Now, I was not having problems with a relationship, but with a guy at work. The quality of his work was good, but the petty cash wasn't adding up, and then some tools went missing. There were also issues with timekeeping. I thought maybe he had a drug problem. I asked spirit several times for guidance. None came!

I kept asking spirit for guidance as the situation worsened and my alarm bells were ringing louder. Eventually, I took matters into my own hands and fired the chap. He didn't take it well, and I felt shaken afterwards.

I took the drive back around the North circular towards my home. The guy had an uncommon Spanish name, Sergio. There on the back of a lorry in front was the guy's name, and below that was a picture of a motorbike. Ah, thank you, spirit, I thought, "On your bike!" That was their way of saying I had done the right thing.

As I crossed the River Thames, I had a few optional routes to get back home. I decided to take the Church Rd hill and up and around to Turners' listed view. This was a view over the Petersham Fields, which often had cattle grazing, and afforded a great view over a curve of the Thames, with the roof of Ham house in the distance. Since Turner had painted the scene, it had become a listed view. I drank in the expanse.

Now, on the other side of the road was a pub. I decided that I deserved a beer after the day I had experienced, and I pulled up and ventured into the pub to then take my drink across the road and admire the view.

As I waited at the bar, the phone rang on the counter; the barman picked up.

"Hello, Sergio," he said.

I held my breath. "There will be a message in this," I thought.

"Your takeaway is ready!" the barman continued and promptly hung up.

"He had taken the tools," I thought.

I took my pint and felt supported by the spirit world. I thought it was funny that they wouldn't tell me before but backed me up afterwards. Of course, this is because spirit won't live our lessons for us. It is all too easy when you have a belief in the spirit world, and so many amazing things do happen, that you can start to rely on them. This isn't usually a healthy thing to do. Spirit knows this and will pull back when they feel that you are beginning to expect them to live your lessons for you.

A month or two after this, I had another experience at Turners' listed view. I had been visiting friends in Kent. This friend had a large garden, and since my previous visit, he had purchased the top of a cathedral spire and placed it in the garden as a focal point to a vista. This gentleman had known loved ones pass away.

Well, a good ten days after the visit, I rounded the bend again at the top of the hill in Richmond. The skies were dark, and rain clouds hung in the air. All was gloomy apart from in the distance; a church spire shone out like a floodlit beacon, where the sun's rays pierced the clouds above it. I remembered my experience sat in my van in Golders Green. I slowed my van right down and peered out. A miracle, I thought.

The following day, I drove the same way as I wanted to investigate my experience. Again, it was a gloomy late afternoon. The spire was nowhere to be seen. I parked up and gazed out. Yes, there it was, a grey spire in the distance. I told my friend about the lit spire as I thought it was a sign from those in heaven. Many months later I happened to drive in that area. I saw the church along the roadside, I peered at the church sign, It was the same as my name!

Baptism

I suppose I was wanting a wider sense of belonging, or was it acceptance, but I thought one day that it would be nice to be baptised. An American medium was often saying that she was a practising Catholic. Perhaps I wanted a level of acceptance; maybe I wanted to feel sanctified. My friends in Kent had just had grandchildren baptised.

Spirit must have been laughing their heads off on heaven's side of life at my thoughts as they hatched a plan!

My bed at home was placed centrally in the room, with one end by the window. In the winter, I slept with my head away from the window to avoid catching a chill, while in the summer, I had my head near the window for fresh air. This isn't something I thought about; I just did it automatically.

One night, I got into bed and did the switch, although it was mid-way through the season. I lay down and, within seconds, was fast asleep. Then, in the middle of the night, I woke and lay there with eyes wide open and alert. Splash, water landed directly on my forehead. How can this be? I'm in my bedroom. I sprang out of bed and turned the light on. Peering up at the ceiling, I could see a droplet. The roof had sprung a leak. I had been baptised!

I then thought it fitting that no person was baptising me, nor any established order! Spirit were reinforcing my sense of belonging to them. God was baptising me!

A Series of Workshops

After what must have been 15 years of demming at the spiritual churches, my area of work broadened. I tried working at fairs but did not think that was for me at all. However, they did offer me a platform to demonstrate in public to others not involved in the spiritual movement. I enjoyed that.

A church asked me if I would run a workshop. This went down well, and I ended up doing one a month. It was not supposed to be a series, but it turned out like that. I realised that I was 'passing on the baton!' I also did some experimental exercises and pushed the boundaries, some with great effect.

We had a great time, and everybody got a lot out of the sessions. From a personal point of view, I found it very rewarding. There was a core of the same people that came each month while others floated in and out.

A Search for Answers

Years before, and sometime after I had joined a class, I went on holiday to Egypt. I had never been drawn to go there previously, but the spiritual people in and around my classes seemed to think there was a lot to see there from a spiritual point of view.

I booked a long trip and stayed at a hostel in Luxor. Not going with a group meant that I was constantly harassed by the locals, trying to sell me something I didn't want. They wouldn't take no for an answer, and after a while, the constant harassment wore thin. I enjoyed going to the Valley of the Kings and Queens and into tombs.

Back in Luxor, I tried to get some peace by renting a felucca, a traditional Egyptian wooden boat with a canvas sail, for a sojourn on the Nile. Even there, they would cry out to you from another boat, "hashish, hashish!" They didn't understand the word NO!

I took a coach trip to Hathor temple. The coach was accompanied by security cars, and we went in convoy. There had been trouble in the past, and the Egyptian government were not taking any chances with their tourist dollar. Dendera was about 40 miles north of Luxor. The local people here were much more polite, and a group of men stood in a row holding out postcards and other souvenirs in the hope of a sale, all lined up outside the temple. After all my experiences, I went there thinking God would show me what I was looking for. This temple was built in 2250 BC and was still incredibly complete. Inside on a ceiling was a huge disc of the zodiac. I was amazed that they had so much knowledge going back such a long way. I wandered around the dusty temple, enjoying the coolness of the temple, a relief from the soaring temperatures outside.

I have to say that although it was an amazing building, I didn't find anything spiritual in there. I came out of the temple into the bright sunshine and heat. "GOD," I asked in my mind, "What am I here to do?" I looked around, but I couldn't see any signs. I don't know what I was expecting! You cannot demand of God, and you cannot stamp your foot!

As I walked back to the postcard sellers, behind them, a woman was going about her chores. She, along with her young son, was struggling to lift a large sack of grain onto the back of a donkey. They tried, and it fell to the ground. The men standing a few feet away selling postcards didn't do a thing. She tried again, but you could see it was too heavy for them both. I walked past the hawkers and up to this Moslem-cloaked woman. I gestured, leant down, put the sack onto the donkey's back and turned for the coach. "Shokran," she said. A nearby man relayed her words: "She says, thank you."

We are all here to serve.

The Pandemic & a Virtual Reality

When COVID was first in the news and purely centred around Wuhan in China, I was filled with a desire to panic buy food. Realising that it was just 'energy', I always resisted. Also, the energy wasn't very dignified! It must have come to me three times whenever I heard the news.

Three months later, we were facing our first lockdown in the UK, and people were panic-buying food. I had to make changes at work and only send out 'safe cells' of staff. We juggled things around, and I managed to keep most of the people employed. As we were working outside, we managed to work safely, only being unable to visit the gardens where one had to go through the owner's house. I kept myself busy throughout.

However, all the Churches were shut. I had a booking just two days before lockdown in Chertsey. The other spiritual churches had already closed. The lady who ran the church had her mother come through and reminded her of the house they used to live in, which had a very large bolt on the door. We all knew what she was getting at! Her daughter had health issues.

After the first lockdown eased, I had a phone call from Wimbledon Church. They had teamed up with a YouTube and Facebook channel and were live-streaming their services. I was asked if I would like to be one of their working mediums. Of course, I jumped at the chance. It was very interesting as there was no congregation. All the recipients were watching from their computer screens in their own homes. As a result, there was a 20-second delay for any feedback or information. This dispelled the accusation of 'cold reading'.

For the first live online event I did, I was 'shaking like a leaf' to start with, and I tried to take comfort from the words my friend Shirley had said: "Everybody in the spirit world knew who was coming to hear the service, who was available to be lined up in the spirit world to give a message and out of all of those, whose energies were compatible with mine so that an accurate message could be given." It was all planned from the spirit side of life. With all that said, it meant that I could relax. Or try to anyway! Anything new is always daunting until it becomes familiar.

That morning, I awoke to the song "The Wombles of Wimbledon", but I couldn't get it out of my head. Even as I made my way to the church, it played over and over like a stuck record. When I walked into the church, I immediately saw a ceramic figure in front of the lectern of a Womble! Apparently, a medium had gifted it to the Robinsons a few weeks before. Immediately, I calmed down as spirit had given me the evidence to say,

"Don't worry, we are with you".

As it happened, it went exceedingly well, and a lot of very specific information came through. Of course, spirit were never going to let me down! If anything, the 20-second delay seemed to help the link, as one had time to get the next piece of information. I was asked back a few times and always enjoyed those virtual sessions. Afterwards, I would get the link by email and send it straight on to an aunt in Australia. Finally, my family could see what I did!

I also emailed it to friends who didn't know that I did that kind of thing. One garden designer friend said she thought I would be 'swaying and chanting' and was surprised that it was 'credible.' Having it on video meant that people could make up their own minds.

A Meeting with Old Friends

Recently, Derek Robinson and Hazel came through to me again. Of all places, I was in a DIY superstore. I was rushing around in my day job, and linking to the spirit world was the last thing on my mind. At first, it was a faint thought of Derek, and it got stronger and stronger as I halted in the aisle. Then Hazel came to me just after Derek. "Why are you here?" I asked with my mind. I didn't hear any words or messages, so I just stood there and enjoyed the meeting. After what must have been 15 seconds, they left. I turned on my heel and carried on down the aisle. Walking back to the checkout, I passed some wind chimes. I sent a message to Derek's grandson.

"Would Derek and Hazel have had windchimes?" I asked, "They have just visited me in a superstore!"

"Yes," he replied, "they did, and whenever I hear them, it reminds me of them!"

It turned out that it was also their anniversary at that time. It was great to be a messenger for this family from people that I once knew.

I watched some American mediums on YouTube, as there are a few who have become quite well-known in the States. One said something which I have thought myself: "I get more excited than the person getting the message!" That was me! I would get so absorbed in it all. Sometimes, I think I know more people in the spirit world than I do living here.

Don't Cry for Me, Argentina

I was booked to work at the North London Spiritualist Church for their Saturday evening of clairvoyance. I had donned my suit and was tuning in. I went to a lady sat in the front row and was bringing her father through strongly. Out of the blue, a spirit man said the words to the song "Don't Cry for Me Argentina "! At the same time that he said it, I also saw in my mind's eye the lady who ran the Clapham Spiritualist Church, whose name was Argentina! Those words came through, so I simply relayed them and paused. The recipient answered me, "I had my suitcases all packed to go to Argentina, but my husband had a heart attack, so I didn't go!" This was an unusual piece of information.

I was friends with Argentina from Clapham Spiritualist Church. A few seasons before, I had been on holiday in Madeira and had sent her photos of a tall ship moored overnight in the bay at Funchal.

Argentina had replied, "I'm on it!" It turned out she was a volunteer crewmember, something that I knew she liked to do.

A few weeks after working at North London, I was booked at Clapham Spiritualist Church. There was a good turnout, and the room was full. Again, I was tuning in and had a connection with Argentina herself, who was sitting within the congregation. I was in the middle of the reading when a spirit man said loudly, again the same words, "Don't cry for me, Argentina!" I assumed immediately the words were from Argentina's late husband, who had passed not more than a year earlier.

Argentina replied, "I had my suitcases all packed to go to Argentina, but my husband had a heart attack, so I couldn't go!" I was gobsmacked at her reply, which was the same word for word as at North London! I carried on with the demonstration. Spirit had certainly got my attention!

As I left the church that night, I mulled over what had happened. I had a feeling Argentina the country was going to be in the news, but I didn't know why. After a few weeks, I forgot about my prediction. It must have been some months later, and the World Cup was on. I heard that Argentina were doing well. I remembered my experience and just knew that they would win the World Cup!

I set about telling friends my prediction! A few asked me if I had placed a bet! I knew they would win.

The day came for the final, and I settled myself into the Pottery Bar opposite my gardening office to enjoy the match. I filled in Lucia, who worked on the other side of the bar, with my prediction. She already knew that I did spirit work. She also asked if I had placed a bet! I told her my story about a dog called Blue from many years earlier and how I had lost £50.00 on a bet, and I knew that I could never bet on something that had been given to me spiritually!

I settled into the football match, very excited and, with a few pints, feeling jubilant! The game was very tense, with Argentina looking like the winners in the first half. Then the other team caught up, and it was a cliffhanger right up to the last moment! Argentina won on a penalty! What a match! Argentina won the game. Journalists wrote that it was the most exciting match in World Cup history. I couldn't believe it! I got very drunk that evening.

Family Feud

I was back at Clapham working. In the middle of a reading, I sensed a gentleman drawing close, and he began to talk to me. I relayed to the recipient, "There was a feud in your family." "Yes," the lady replied. "This was a long, long time ago." "Yes," came back the reply.

"This feud was caused by a man who has been in the spirit world for a long time," I said. "Yes, my grandfather", the lady replied. Well, since he has been in the spirit world, it may have taken him a long time, but he realises now that 'life is too short' and that he was wrong to create the feud. He whispers an apology to you, and he acknowledges it now that he was in the wrong. "Thank you," the lady quietly replied.

Three times now, I have given a reading where a father has said that a son hasn't attended his own father's funeral. Spirit showed me the coffin lopsided with only three pallbearers! Each time, the man in the spirit world has been really upset that his own flesh and blood had not shown up to pay their respects. One of these fathers acknowledged that there had been a rift between them in life, but he didn't think that their differences were so great that his son shouldn't show up to his funeral.

Love and life are hardly ever perfect, and when it really matters, people can put their differences aside and behave in a better way.

A Birthday Present

During the busy gardening season, in May, it is 'bedding out'. This is where annual flowers are planted in the garden. This task makes it an especially busy period as the design, landscape, and regular maintenance are all in full swing.

By late June, I was approaching burnout, so I booked a short break in Madeira again to recharge my batteries. I booked a day trip excursion online for the middle day, which happened to be on my birthday. It being my third trip there, I knew how popular it could get, and unless I booked in advance, I might not get anything at all when on the island. The advertisement showed a picture of an arch of stone overlooking the sea. It looked as though one could go swimming in a sea cave! It drew me in, and I booked it.

I arrived in the apartment I had taken overlooking a town square in the old quarter and soaked up the island atmosphere on the first day. The next day, I waited a few yards from the accommodation at the designated collection point. On time, a Land Rover arrived, and I was off for my day's excursion. We stopped at other hotels, and before long, the vehicle was full of other tourists. We drove out of the city and along the winding roads to a lookout point on a cliff. It was warm, and I could smell the eucalyptus oil in the air. It reminded me of Australia.

The next part of the trip, the driver unexpectedly took us onto what were little more than tracks. He whizzed along, and it began to feel more like a rally drive! I loved it. The driver was a great character and a bit of a daredevil. "Look to the left, everyone", and as tourists, we all obeyed, with our rubber necks! Whereupon he took a sharp right down a steep hill! We all laughed as it became a roller coaster ride! This broke the ice with the group.

We drove down to the seaside and zigzagged our way to the sea cave. We bundled out of the Land Rover and made our way along the track. The arch of stone was nice, but it was no swimming hole, and a wall of rock had been built across to hold the water in, making it look like a part of the sea on the internet picture.

Back in the jeep, we headed across the island to the other side. Here, we had an hour free to swim in a natural pool area. The sea itself was far too rough to swim in, and the waves would sometimes break over the rock wall and into the pool. This was the colder and wetter side of the island and where the locals and tourists alike would go for a swim. I put my towel on a rock and ventured into the water. It was great to go for a swim in the clean, salty water. I felt refreshed. I swam to the other side of the pool and climbed up onto the rock sea wall. I stood up and took a few steps along it. Immediately, I noticed an enormous crab on the other side of the rock. It shrank back a little as it saw me. I stood still. I had an instant knowing that the crab would come to me. I stood motionless.

The crab peered up at me and, sure enough, edged its way to me. I didn't move a muscle. It climbed onto my foot! It was so big that my foot was covered with crab! A man walked towards me from the other side of the wall. He was from a family group in the same Land Rover. He looked at me and looked down at the crab. Startled, the crab moved away.

"It knows you won't hurt it, "he said. "No!" I answered. "It is my birthday today, and it is a present from the universe! I am a Cancerian!"

I wanted to say that it was a present from my mother, but realised I was being wacky enough in the eyes of the stranger. I laughed and dived back into the pool!

I had gone on the holiday alone and was aware I was the only lone traveller for that day's excursion. This experience was the best present I could ever have had.

Our next port of call was magical, too. We drove up into the highlands, and the guide announced that we would be visiting a 'fog forest'. We soon drove into some cold fog, in stark contrast to the bright sunny day from moments earlier. We set off into the fog on foot. I was speechless; there were moss-covered trees of ancient laurel standing eerily in the fog. This place really did feel magical. I made a mental note to return someday so that I could explore the forest properly. If Tolkien got his inspiration for Fangorn Forest here I wouldn't be surprised!

At our next stop, we had lunch at a cafe, and the group all sat at the same table. The family group sat next to me. The family man must have told his wife and daughter about the crab as the lady quizzed me. I answered honestly that I had come alone as I had been working so hard that I had badly needed a break. I take photos of wildlife, she told me and showed me her Instagram page. We exchanged details and then followed each other.

At a pit stop later in the day, I tried my luck to see if a bird would eat some biscuit out of my hand! The guide spotted this and made great fun out of me. He was a character. I think the family man took further note.

Further along in the day, we were driving along the coast. I felt my mother around me strongly. I looked across, and there were some large rocks rising out of the sea. I was reminded of the 'Three Sisters' in Tasmania, which were three rocks in the sea. I turned to the guide, "What are those stones called?" I asked as I felt my mother prompt me, "What?" He replied. "What are those stones in the water called?" I repeated, pointing towards the rocks. The guide became very excited, "My name, my name!" He exclaimed. By coincidence, his surname was the same as the rock! The family man gave me a strange look. The day was turning into quite an experience.

Nearing the end of the trip, I turned to the family man, what are your plans for the rest of the holiday? He looked nervous. I realised I had spooked him. I repeated the question. "We were hoping to walk the peaks, but my wife doesn't like walking," he said. On an earlier trip, I had done that walk, I told him, the views are so breath-taking they make your legs move! Another couple in the group had done the walk the day before and agreed to that. I didn't find out if they took the walk. We exchanged broad smiles as we said our goodbyes.

I had one more day in Madeira. It had done the trick, and my batteries were recharged.

January 19th, 2024

Seven years had passed since my mother departed to life's higher side.

I had started to visit Tasmania annually each English winter. This was to see my father and sister, as well as to get some winter sunshine in my quiet time.

This visit happened to coincide with a psychic fair in my hometown and, on the weekend before, in another town. The organiser kindly let me work there as a reader again. We agreed that I could do an evening demonstration of clairvoyance in both towns. I did flower readings, and the evening was advertised that you bring along a flower in a paper bag so that I wouldn't know who I was reading. I hadn't thought through the wording of the advert properly, realising that everyone attending would be expecting a reading!

The first evening went very well, and there was a mixture of clear spirit and psychic readings. The only problem was that the evening went on for a lot longer than expected, to give a reading to everybody. The following weekend, the organiser urged me to read faster. This was good advice, and double the number of people came along. Again, I felt obliged to read for everyone! There were over 30 paper bags in front of me. Quite a mountain of paper bags!

It was a fantastic evening, and the information flowed. At the start of the evening, I said that if anyone didn't get their flower reading, I would be happy to give them their money back. Nobody asked. The people attending were a very nice group, and again, a mixture of information came through on a lot of different levels.

I took from a bag the smallest pink flower. A baby lost to spirit came through for one young man, with spirit assuring him that the little one was with an older relative spirit side. The older relative, a grandmother, gave me her 'calling card', a jewellery box that played music when the lid was lifted.

Someone then pushed me physically in the back. They are pushing you forward, I said. He accepted that he had felt a push in the back himself; he had turned around, and nobody was there. He had his evidence and assurance that it was now time to heal, let go and move on.

Next came a hollyhock and a positive psychic message. "You will go for a job interview, and you will get the job!" I joked that I would soon be on a plane, and she would not be able to find me if I had got that wrong! I got the job today, she said, everybody laughed.

A rose flower later, a lass's Gran came through, and she told me how she would set the table and say Grace before the meal. This seemed to be trivial information, but I never question what the spirit people want me to say if it is impressed upon me. Then the girls' dog came through. The dog had been a great part of the girl's life, and she had deeply mourned the loss as much as if it were a person. With an Iris bloom, I picked up a healing path for a lady; various psychic information came through, and I received a lot of head nodding in affirmation. You have wondered about who you were in a past life? I felt compelled to ask. Yes, was answered, so spirit proceeded to tell her she had been around at the times of Jesus and had lived in those same parts. She had lived a simple, wholesome life, and she had carried this simplicity through in this life. People in this life who were too clever or too complex, she steered clear from. In this life, she needed simplicity. The lady agreed.

A relative dropped in and said he was a fisherman. The lady confirmed. Cast your net wider, spirit said to this lady. I thought this was also Jesus-like, and the message was that she needed to expand her horizons and her way of thinking.

Several more flowers were read. A biker came through for one girl and said his life had been cut short. He went on to say that he liked the music that was played at his funeral! I asked the girl if something had been moved in her home and that it was him who moved it. She agreed and said she had wondered! Then it was a nigella flower. "You walk the land, your father walked the land." The young lady nodded; a lot of people try to force it, I said, but with you, it comes naturally.

Spirit then talked about art, working with bark; suddenly, I saw an aborigine and felt earth pressed into their face. The lady understood. You are 'of the land,' she nodded. She was part Aboriginal and her Aboriginal ancestor was communicating. I was amazed, and I felt honoured. The soil must have been ochre, which was sacred to the Aborigines. I saw the Aborigine for a fraction of a second, and it came with a sacred feeling as the ochre was rubbed into the skin.

An abelia flower was picked next, followed by a variety of roses and dahlias; an incredible array of different flowers and an equal array of information flowed. As the evening drew on, I started to get tired, and my energy was dropping. I marvelled how spirit still managed to come through at the end to prove themselves and to give healing. My energy had dwindled, and as the evening started at six and it was now nearly nine pm, I felt flat now reading the flowers.

I opened up another paper bag and linked to a different flower to the one that I was holding in my hand, an antirrhinum, commonly called a 'snapdragon'. "Who has been snappy around you?" I asked. "No one." The lady looked at me blankly. I went back to spirit. They gave me the message: you have been to a grave recently and put flowers on it. "Yes," she replied.

“This woman was ‘snappy’ before she passed away?’ I asked, "Yes," the lady said.

The spirit said, "I'm sorry. It wasn't the real me; I was not myself. I am sorry for being snappy to you; you didn't deserve those words." The recipient wiped a silent tear from her eye and nodded.

I had done my job. It was a great success.

The following day I spent with my sister. We revisited Goat Island, a tidal island where we had played as children.

The day after, I was due to do one-to-one sittings at the psychic spiritual fair in my hometown to follow on from my evening of clairvoyance with flowers. I felt out of sorts that morning as I awoke, so to rebalance my energies, I took myself off to the Bluff.

With an early morning coffee on the dash, bread and 'avo toast', I parked up at the Bluff. I walked to the Aborigine rock carvings and filled my lungs with the fresh air. As I came to the lighthouse, I noticed something at its base. I walked closer. There was a flower. For once, I didn't know what variety it was! There it was, lying on the gravel in front of the lighthouse. This was my present from the spirit world!

It was for all my hard work. I thanked the spirit people with my mind. I had needed a boost, and this was it. They were telling me that I had been like a lighthouse with my spirit work.

The Last Day of my Holiday in Early 2024 Approached

I had arranged to see my father and his wife on that day, and we had agreed to visit a community centre. As they were now living in a care home, they might meet people that they had known from their region previously. We arrived on time, and there was a great spread of savouries and sweets for all the attendees. I eyed up the blackberry jam on scones with cream! We all three devoured accordingly when the time was right! Sadly, there was no one there that they knew, but I thought at least I had got them out of the care home for the day.

We then went for a drive, and I took them to where my father had once moored his yacht. We then drove on to the coast, to Greens Beach, had a short walk and then ordered a simple lunch of toasted sandwiches at the corner store.

Returning to the care home, my father had other ideas already planned and directed me to the right, down an unsurfaced road. I didn't question him, and knowing that I was his taxi for the day, I kept on driving. As we neared the Narawntapu National Park, the land became poorer and poorer; my dad beckoned me into a farm gate, "Keep Out", it read.

We drove through and up to the farmstead. Dad got out and disappeared for a minute or two before others appeared and beckoned me and Dad's wife, Beryl, out into their warm home. These were old friends of Dad's. Apparently, they had connections to Flinders Island, too. We went into their house. Like Dad and his partner, they were in their eighties. They were holding on to their farm and their independent lives. In Australia, it is quite acceptable to drop into people you know with little or no notice. In the UK, everything would have to be by appointment!

We then travelled back along the gravel road, my father again pointing up to a stranger's driveway. I obeyed, and we met other friends of theirs. I realised that my dad might have thought that he would not see these friends again, so I was very glad to be the driver for the day.

As we drove back from Greens Beach to Beaconsfield, it was a mixture of farmland and bush. As the car turned the corner, there standing beside the road, in broad daylight, was a kangaroo! This was unusual as they are nocturnal. This one was different; it was snow white, an albino!

It was a magical moment, and I quickly pulled the car over while pointing it out in amazement. "Look, a white kangaroo!"

He hopped off into the bush. Excitedly, I fumbled for my phone's camera and said, "Wait here, I'll be back in a minute." I dashed off as fast as I could after the kangaroo! I sprinted through the clearing and got my phone onto camera. I took a few photos of the kangaroo.

I felt so blessed to see the white kangaroo, like a wise aboriginal elder, gazing at me and giving me a blessing for the work that I had done there.

I felt that I had passed life's tests and initiations to at last fully embrace the work I was about to do.

Life had made me a medium.

The End

APPENDIX

The College of Psychic Studies
16 Queensberry Place, London, SW7 2EB UK
www.collegeofpsychicstudies.co.uk

Insight and Intuition International
www.insightandintuition.com

SAGB - The Spiritualist Association of Great Britain
341 Queenstown Road, Battersea, London SW8 4LH UK
www.sagb.org.uk

SNU - The Spiritualist National Union
www.snu.org.uk

List of SNU spiritualist churches throughout the UK
www.snu.org.uk/Pages/Events/Category/churches

The Arthur Findlay College (part of the SNU)
Stansted Hall, Stansted Mountfitchet, Essex CM24 8UD UK
www.arthurfindlaycollege.org

Clapham Spiritualist Church

11a North Street, Old Town, Clapham, London SW4 0HN UK

www.snu.org.uk/clapham-spiritualist-church

Kingston Spiritualist Church

Villiers Road, Kingston, Surrey KT1 3AR UK

www.kingstonsc.net

Richmond Spiritualist Church

97 Church Road, Richmond, Surrey TW10 6LU UK

www.snu.org.uk/richmond-spiritualist-church

Wimbledon Spiritualist Church

136 Hartfield Road, Wimbledon London SW19 3TG UK

www.wimbledonspiritualistchurch.co.uk

Dr Jason Betts - Psychic events

Tasmania, Australia www.emeraldalchemy.com

ABOUT THE AUTHOR

Jeff Hewitt has spent a couple of decades navigating the nuanced realms of the unseen, offering guidance and insight with his psychic abilities. With a compassionate heart and a deep connection to the spiritual world, Jeff has dedicated his life to helping others find clarity, healing, and direction. His journey into the depths of both human and spiritual experience has not only transformed his own life but also the lives of countless individuals who have sought his counsel.

As a natural medium, Jeff possesses a rare gift to communicate beyond the physical, offering messages of hope and reconciliation from the spiritual world. His work transcends conventional boundaries, providing a bridge between the here and the beyond. Jeff's approach is grounded in honesty, integrity, and a profound respect for the sacredness of his work.

In his autobiography, Jeff shares not only his journey into becoming a medium but also his insights into the spiritual dimensions that influence our daily lives. Through his narrative, readers will discover the transformative power of spiritual awareness and the potential within themselves to connect with the unseen.

FURTHER INFORMATION

Jeff extends his service through a website. Here, individuals can find information on private readings, workshops, and other resources designed to encourage healing and spiritual growth.

www.JeffHewittMedium.com

Printed in Great Britain
by Amazon

43204296R00136